Mastering Non-Functional Requirements

Analysis, architecture, and assessment

Sameer Paradkar

BIRMINGHAM - MUMBAI

Mastering Non-Functional Requirements

First published: May 2017

Production reference: 1150517

Published by Packt Publishing Ltd.
Livery Place
35 Livery Street
Birmingham
B3 2PB, UK.
ISBN 978-1-78829-923-7

www.packtpub.com

Credits

Author
Sameer Paradkar

Reviewer
James D. Miller

Commissioning Editor
Merint Mathew

Acquisition Editor
Karan Sadawana

Content Development Editor
 Amrita Noronha

Technical Editor
Deepti Tuscano

Copy Editor
Safis Editing

Project Coordinator
Shweta H Birwatkar

Proofreader
Safis Editing

Indexer
Tejal Daruwale Soni

Graphics
Tania Dutta

Production Coordinator
Deepika Naik

About the Author

Sameer Paradkar is an enterprise architect with 15+ years of solid experience in the ICT industry which spans across consulting, systems integration, and product development. He is an Open Group TOGAF, Oracle Master Java EA, TMForum NGOSS, IBM SOA Solutions, IBM Cloud Solutions, IBM MobileFirst, ITIL Foundation V3 and COBIT 5 certified enterprise architect. He serves as an advisory architect on enterprise architecture programs and continues to work as a subject matter expert. He has worked on multiple architecture transformations and modernization engagements in the USA, UK, Europe, Asia Pacific and the Middle East Regions that presented a phased roadmap to the transformation that maximized the business value while minimizing risks and costs.

Sameer is part of IT Strategy and Transformation Practice in AtoS. Prior to AtoS, he has worked in organizations such as EY - IT Advisory, IBM GBS, Wipro Consulting Services, Tech Mahindra, and Infosys Technologies and specializes in IT strategies and enterprise transformation engagements.

I would like to dedicate this book to my wife, family members and friends for their encouragement, support and love.

Many people throughout my career have directly and indirectly contributed to this book. I would like to take this opportunity to acknowledge their contribution, influence, and inspiration. I believe I am lucky to have found opportunities to work with extremely talented and exceptions individuals who extended their wholehearted support throughout my career. My eternal thanks to them for believing in me and providing exciting opportunities. I would like to thank my team members, chief and lead architects, mentors, discussion partners, reviewers, and supporters, whose valuable comments and feedback have significantly contributed to this book. I look forward to your comments and valuable inputs on an on-going basis. I would like to recognize and thank my current and former colleagues who made my corporate journey exciting, enriching and fulfilling.

About the Reviewer

James D. Miller is an IBM certified expert, creative innovator and accomplished Director, Sr. Project Leader and Application/System Architect with +35 years of extensive applications and system design and development experience across multiple platforms and technologies. Experiences include introducing customers to new and sometimes disruptive technologies and platforms, integrating with IBM Watson Analytics, Cognos BI, TM1 and Web architecture design, systems analysis, GUI design and testing, Database modelling and systems analysis, design, and development of OLAP, client/server, web and mainframe applications and systems utilizing; IBM Watson Analytics, IBM Cognos BI and TM1 (TM1 rules, TI, TM1Web and Planning Manager), Cognos Framework Manager, dynaSight-- ArcPlan, ASP, DHTML, XML, IIS, MS Visual Basic and VBA, Visual Studio, PERL, SPLUNK, WebSuite, MS SQL Server, ORACLE, SYBASE Server, and so on.

Responsibilities have also included all aspects of Windows and SQL solution development and design including: analysis; GUI (and Web site) design; data modelling; table, screen/form and script development; SQL (and remote stored procedures and triggers) development/testing; test preparation and management and training of programming staff. Other experience includes development of ETL infrastructure such as data transfer automation between mainframe (DB2, Lawson, Great Plains, and so on) systems and client/server SQL server and Web based applications and integration of enterprise applications and data sources.

Mr. Miller has acted as Internet Applications Development manager responsible for the design, development, QA and delivery of multiple Web Sites including online trading applications, warehouse process control and scheduling systems, administrative and control applications. Mr. Miller also was responsible for the design, development and administration of a Web based financial reporting system for a 450 million dollar organization, reporting directly to the CFO and his executive team.

Mr. Miller has also been responsible for managing and directing multiple resources in various management roles including project and team leader, lead developer and applications development director.

Jim has authored *Cognos TM1 Developers Certification Guide, Mastering Splunk, Learning IBM Watson Analytics* and a number of whitepapers on best practices such as *Establishing a Center of Excellence* and continues to post blogs on a number of relevant topics based upon personal experiences and industry best practices.

Jim is a perpetual learner continuing to pursue experiences and certifications, currently holding the following current technical certifications:

IBM Certified Business Analyst - Cognos TM1

IBM Cognos TM1 Master 385 Certification (perfect score 100% on exam)

IBM Certified Advanced Solution Expert - Cognos TM1

IBM Cognos TM1 10.1 Administrator Certification C2020-703 (perfect score 100% on exam)

IBM OpenPages Developer Fundamentals C2020-001-ENU (98% on exam)

IBM Cognos 10 BI Administrator C2020-622 (98% on exam)

IBM Cognos 10 BI Professional C2020-180

Specialties: The evaluation and introduction of innovative and disruptive technologies, Cloud migration, IBM Watson Analytics, Big Data, Data Visualizations, Cognos BI and TM1 application Design and Development, OLAP, Visual Basic, SQL Server, Forecasting and Planning; International Application Development, Business Intelligence, Project Development and Delivery and process improvement.

I would like to thank Nanette L. Miller who is always on my mind and always in my heart…

www.PacktPub.com

For support files and downloads related to your book, please visit www.PacktPub.com.

Did you know that Packt offers eBook versions of every book published, with PDF and ePub files available? You can upgrade to the eBook version at www.PacktPub.com and as a print book customer, you are entitled to a discount on the eBook copy. Get in touch with us at service@packtpub.com for more details.

At www.PacktPub.com, you can also read a collection of free technical articles, sign up for a range of free newsletters and receive exclusive discounts and offers on Packt books and eBooks.

https://www.packtpub.com/mapt

Get the most in-demand software skills with Mapt. Mapt gives you full access to all Packt books and video courses, as well as industry-leading tools to help you plan your personal development and advance your career.

Why subscribe?

- Fully searchable across every book published by Packt
- Copy and paste, print, and bookmark content
- On demand and accessible via a web browser

Customer Feedback

Thanks for purchasing this Packt book. At Packt, quality is at the heart of our editorial process. To help us improve, please leave us an honest review on this book's Amazon page at `https://www.amazon.com/dp/178829923X`.

If you'd like to join our team of regular reviewers, you can e-mail us at `customerreviews@packtpub.com`. We award our regular reviewers with free eBooks and videos in exchange for their valuable feedback. Help us be relentless in improving our products!

Table of Contents

Preface

Maintaining software is hard and therefore expensive and IT departments are often under funded. However, if they are in a *just do it* mode then non-functional requirements are easy to be forgotten. The consequences of leaving these NFRs lead directly to the aforementioned maintenance problems and increased technical debt.

NFRs are necessary to completing the story of the IT application. While you might consider two or three important NFRs (like performance and security), you'll probably not cover the others extensively enough, or you might miss out on them all together. And if you do allocate time to deal with them, when the project schedule slips, the NFRs may be the first thing to get drop. So, whether you plan for NFRs or not, chances are high you won't cover them 100% of the time. You should try to avoid adding technical debt and maintenance nightmares to your future portfolio.

NFRs are key to any software/IT program. They cannot be overlooked or ignored. The book provides a comprehensive approach from analysis, architecture and measurement of non-functional requirements. The book outlines the methodology for capturing the NFRs and also describes a taxonomy framework that can leveraged by analyst and architects for tackling NFRs on engagements.

To summarize, the key differentiators for the book are:

- Covers all the three stages of non-functional requirements that is, analysis, architecture and measurement.
- NFR framework and taxonomy provides guidance around the modelling phase for the NFRs
- Describes the process for capturing and analyzing the KPI and KRAs. These are the key metrics that are required by different stakeholders.
- Trade-offs between various NFRs are covered as part of the title
- Describes the application performance management domain which is a key practice for managing and monitoring of enterprise applications that helps monitor and analyze NFR KPIs and KRAs as part of the ongoing process.

Coverage of the book:

- This book covers areas pertaining to analysis, architecture and measurement of non-functional requirements. A topic with-out which software systems cannot be build or deployed. NFRs are a life-line of any software application and capturing and addressing them is a critical activity in any IT project. The topic in itself is very critical and applicable for IT systems/applications for various industry verticals. The book provides a comprehensive approach from analysis, architecture and measurement of non-functional requirements.

Part I - Analysis:

- The books provides and introduction of NFRs and why NFRs are a critical for building software systems. The next section describes the taxonomy of NFRs that is, scalability, availability, reliability and so on. The books outlines various methodology for capturing the NFRs, The books also outlines and describes a framework that can leveraged by analyst and architects for tackling NFRs for various engagements. The framework will focus on the KPIs and KRA for each of the NFRs which will be the key input for solution design phase. The NRF framework will focus on the most critical NFRs applicable for any given situation and any industry.

Part II - Architecture:

- This section focus on the solution part of the NFRs providing insights into how they will be addressed in the solution design phase. The book covers key NFRs that are most critical for any project and for each NFR provides the various alternatives pertaining to the solution, the design principle that needs to be applied to achieve the desired outcome for example, high availability or scalability or reliability as covered. The book includes considerations for bespoke (Java, .NET) and COTS applications and are applicable to any IT applications/systems in different domains.

Part III - Assessment:

- This part deals with the measurement of NFRs. This outlines the methodology for NFRs measurement. This sections also describes the trade-offs between various NFRs and the best practices to be applied on engagements.

What this book covers

Chapter 1, *Understanding NFRs*, the chapter provides and introduction of NFRs and why NFRs are a critical for building software systems. The chapter also explains the various KPI for each of the key of NFRs that is, scalability, availability, reliability and so on. The book covers the most critical 24 NFRs that are applicable for IT applications and systems.

Chapter 2, *Taxonomy and Framework for NFRs*, this chapter describes the taxonomy of NFRs that is, scalability, availability, reliability and so on. The chapter outlines entire life cycle of NFRs, The chapter describes a framework that can leveraged by business analyst and architects for discovering NFRs on various engagements. The framework will focus on the KPIs and KRA for each of the NFRs which will be the critical input for the solution design phase.

Chapter 3, *Methodology Eliciting - Non Functional Requirements*, this chapter outlines methodology for discovering (elicitations) NFRs. The chapter describes a framework that can be leveraged by business analyst for elicitations of NFRs. The chapter also outlines a framework for prioritization of NFRs. The output of this stage will be the critical input for the solution architecture phase.

Chapter 4, *Solutions Addressing NFRs*, this chapter outlines the solutioning part of the NFRs providing insights, guidance and principles for architecting NFRs. The book covers all the key NFRs that are critical for any project and for each NFR provides the various alternatives pertaining to the solutioning and the design principles that need to be applied to achieve the desired outcome for example, high availability or scalability or reliability and so on. The book includes considerations for bespoke (Java, .Net) and COTS applications and are applicable to any IT applications/systems in different domains.

Chapter 5, *Architectural Patterns and its Impact on NFRs*, this chapter outlines the patterns for NFRs providing insights into architecting NFRs. The chapter covers all the key tiers / layers that are critical for any project and describes various patterns pertaining to the business, database and integration tiers. This also covers impact on various NFRs. This chapter describes the trade-offs between various NFRs and the best practices to be applied on engagements.

Chapter 6, *Sizing, Measurement and Monitoring*, this chapter deals with the measurement of NFRs. This outlines four methodologies for NFRs monitoring and measurement. These include sizing, analytical modelling, quality assurance and monitoring and management. This chapter also describes the approach in depth for monitoring and measuring NFRs.

Chapter 7, *Understanding Pivotal NFRs and Closing Thoughts*, this chapter provides an introduction to the pivotal NFRs. The chapter explains the various KPI for each of the pivotal NFRs. This is the final chapter of the book and provides summary and trends for the NFR domain. This also outlines architecture assessment and NFR measurement methodology.

Who this book is for

The primary audiences for this title are the gamut of roles starting from IT consultant to Chief Architect who are responsible to deliver strategic, tactical and operational engagements for fortune 100 customers worldwide. Non-functional requirements are the key to any software/IT program. They cannot be overlooked or ignored. The book provides a comprehensive approach from analysis, architecture and measurement of non-functional requirements. The book includes considerations for bespoke (Java, .Net and COTS applications). These are applicable to IT applications from various domains. The book outlines the methodology for capturing the NFRs and also describes a framework that can leveraged by analyst and architects for tackling NFRs for various engagements. The audiences for this book include:

- Business Analyst
- Enterprise Architects
- Business Architects
- Solution Architects
- Technical Architects/Designers
- Domain/Security/Integration Architects
- Software Developers, Support Engineers & Test Engineers
- Technical Project Managers
- Project Leads/Technical Leads/Technical Project Managers
- Students - Computer Science/IT Stream

Conventions

In this book, you will find a number of text styles that distinguish between different kinds of information. Here are some examples of these styles and an explanation of their meaning.

New terms and **important words** are shown in bold.

Warnings or important notes appear in a box like this.

 Tips and tricks appear like this.

Reader feedback

Feedback from our readers is always welcome. Let us know what you think about this book-what you liked or disliked. Reader feedback is important for us as it helps us develop titles that you will really get the most out of.

To send us general feedback, simply e-mail `feedback@packtpub.com`, and mention the book's title in the subject of your message.

If there is a topic that you have expertise in and you are interested in either writing or contributing to a book, see our author guide at `www.packtpub.com/authors`.

Customer support

Now that you are the proud owner of a Packt book, we have a number of things to help you to get the most from your purchase.

Errata

Although we have taken every care to ensure the accuracy of our content, mistakes do happen. If you find a mistake in one of our books-maybe a mistake in the text or the code-we would be grateful if you could report this to us. By doing so, you can save other readers from frustration and help us improve subsequent versions of this book. If you find any errata, please report them by visiting `http://www.packtpub.com/submit-errata`, selecting your book, clicking on the **Errata Submission Form** link, and entering the details of your errata. Once your errata are verified, your submission will be accepted and the errata will be uploaded to our website or added to any list of existing errata under the Errata section of that title.

To view the previously submitted errata, go to `https://www.packtpub.com/books/content/support` and enter the name of the book in the search field. The required information will appear under the **Errata** section.

Piracy

Piracy of copyrighted material on the Internet is an ongoing problem across all media. At Packt, we take the protection of our copyright and licenses very seriously. If you come across any illegal copies of our works in any form on the Internet, please provide us with the location address or website name immediately so that we can pursue a remedy.

Please contact us at `copyright@packtpub.com` with a link to the suspected pirated material.

We appreciate your help in protecting our authors and our ability to bring you valuable content.

Questions

If you have a problem with any aspect of this book, you can contact us at `questions@packtpub.com`, and we will do our best to address the problem.

1
Understanding NFRs

The non-functional requirements are those aspects of the IT system that, while not directly affecting the business functionality of the application but have a profound impact on the efficiency and effectiveness of business systems for end users, as well as the people responsible for supporting the program.

The definition of these requirements is an essential factor in developing a total customer solution that delivers business goals. The **non-functional requirements** (**NFRs**) are used primarily to drive the operational aspects of the architecture; in other words, to address major operational and technical areas of the system to ensure the robustness and ruggedness of the application.

Benchmark or **proof of concept** (**POC**) can be used to verify if the implementation meets these requirements or to indicate if a corrective action is necessary. Ideally, a series of tests should be planned that maps to the development schedule and grows in complexity.

The topics that are covered in this chapter are as follows:

- Definition of NFRs
- NFR KPI and metrics

Introducing NFRs

The following pointers state the definition of NFRs:

- To define requirements and constraints on the IT system
- As a basis for cost estimates and early system sizing
- To assess the viability of the proposed IT system
- As an important determining factor of the architecture and design of the operational models
- As a guideline to design phase to meet NFRs such as performance, scalability, and availability

The NFRs for each of the domains, for example, scalability, availability, and so on, must be understood to facilitate the design and development of the target operating model. These include the servers, networks, and platforms including the application runtime environments. These are critical for the execution of benchmark tests. They also affect the design of technical and application components.

End users have expectations about the effectiveness of the application. These characteristics include ease of software use, speed, reliability, and recoverability when unexpected conditions arise. The NFRs define these aspects of the IT system.

The NFRs should be defined precisely and this involves quantifying them. NFRs should provide measurements which the application must meet. For example, the maximum number of time allowed to execute a process, the number of hours in a day an application must be available, the maximum size of a database on disk, and the number of concurrent users supported are typical NFRs the software must implement.

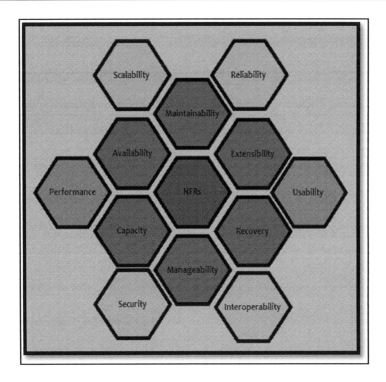

Figure 1: Key non-functional requirements

There are many kinds of non-functional requirements.

Performance

Performance is the responsiveness of the application to perform specific actions in a given time span. Performance is scored in terms of throughput or latency. Latency is the time taken by the application to respond to an event. Throughput is the number of events scored in a given time interval. An application's performance can directly impact its scalability. Enhancing an application's performance often enhances scalability by reducing contention for shared resources.

Performance attributes specify the timing characteristics of the application. Certain features are more time-sensitive than others; the NFRs should identify such software tasks that have constraints on their performance. Response time relates to the time needed to complete specific business processes, batch or interactive, within the target business system.

The system must be designed to fulfill the agreed upon response time requirements, while supporting the defined workload mapped against the given static baseline, on a system platform that does not exceed the stated utilization.

The following attributes are:

- **Throughput**: The ability of the system to execute a given number of transactions within a given unit of time
- **Response times**: The distribution of time which the system takes to respond to the request

Scalability

Scalability is the ability to handle an increase in the workload without impacting the performance, or the ability to quickly expand the architecture.

It is the ability to expand the architecture to accommodate more users, more processes, more transactions, and additional systems and services as the business requirements change and the systems evolve to meet the future business demands. This permits existing systems to be extended without replacing them. This directly affects the architecture and the selection of software components and hardware.

The solution must allow the hardware and the deployed software services and components to be scaled horizontally as well as vertically. Horizontal scaling involves replicating the same functionality across additional nodes; vertical scaling involves the same functionality across bigger and more powerful nodes. Scalability definitions measure volumes of users and data which the system should support.

There are two key techniques for improving both vertical and horizontal scalability:

- Vertical scaling is also known as **scaling up** and includes adding more resources such as memory, CPU, and hard disk to a system
- Horizontal scaling is also known as **scaling out** and includes adding more nodes to a cluster for workload sharing

The following attributes are:

- **Throughput**: Number of maximum transactions your system needs to handle for example, a thousand a day or a million
- **Storage**: Amount of data you are going to need to store
- **Growth requirements**: Data growth in the next 3-5 years

Availability

Availability is the time frame in which the system functions normally and without failures. Availability is measured as the percentage of total application downtime over a defined time period. Availability is affected by failures, exceptions, infrastructure issues, malicious attacks, and maintenance and upgrades.

It is the uptime or the amount of time the system is operational and available for use. This is specified because some systems are architected with expected downtime for activities like database upgrades and backups.

Availability also conveys the number of hours or days per week or weeks per year the application will be available to its end customers, as well as how rapidly it can recover from faults. Since the architecture establishes software, hardware, and networking entities, this requirement extends to all of them. Hardware availability, recoverability, and reliability definitions measure system uptime.

For example, it is specified in terms of **Mean Time Between Failures (MTBF)**.

The following attributes are:

- **Availability**: Application availability considering the weekends, holidays, and maintenance times and failures
- **Locations of operation**: Geographic location, connection requirements, and if the restrictions of the network prevail
- **Offline requirement**: Time available for offline operations including batch processing and system maintenance
- **Length of time between failures**: This is the predicted elapsed time between inherent failures of a system during operation
- **Recoverability**: Time required by the system to resume operation in the event of failure
- **Resilience**: The reliability characteristics of the system and sub-components

Capacity

This NFR defines the ways in which the system is expected to scale-up by increasing capacity, hardware, or adding machines based on business objectives.

Capacity is delivering enough functionality required for the end users. A request for a web service to provide 1,000 requests per second when the server is only capable of 100 requests a second, may not succeed. While this sounds like an availability issue, it occurs because the server is unable to handle the requisite capacity.

A single node may not be able to provide enough capacity, and one needs to deploy multiple nodes with a similar configuration to meet organizational capacity requirements. Capacity to identify a failing node and restart it on another machine or VM is a NFR.

The following attributes are:

- Throughput is the number of peak transactions the system needs to handle
- Storage is the volume of data the system can persist at runtime to disk and relates to the memory/disk
- Year-on-year growth requirements (users, processing, and storage)
- The e-channel growth projections
- Different types of things (for example, activities or transactions supported, and so on)
- For each type of transaction, volumes on an hourly, daily, weekly, monthly basis, and so on
- During the specific time of the day (for example, at lunch), week, month, or year are volumes significantly higher
- Transaction volume growth expected and additional volumes you will be able to handle

Security

Security is the ability of an application to avoid malicious incidences and events outside of the designed system usage, and prevent disclosure or loss of information. Improving security increases the reliability of an application by reducing the likelihood of an attack succeeding and impairing operations. Adding security controls protects assets and prevents unauthorized access and manipulation of critical information. The factors that affect an application security are confidentiality and integrity. The key security controls used to secure systems are authorization, authentication, encryption, auditing, and logging.

Definition and monitoring of effectiveness in meeting the security requirements of the system, for example, to avoid financial harm in accounting systems, is critical. Integrity requirements restrict access to functionality or data to certain users, and protect the privacy of data entered into the software.

The following attributes are:

- **Authentication**: Correct identification of parties attempting to access systems and protection of systems from unauthorized parties
- **Authorization**: Mechanism required to authorize users to perform different functions within the systems
- **Encryption (data at rest or data in flight)**: All external communications between the data server and clients must be encrypted
- **Data confidentiality**: All data must be protectively marked, stored, and protected
- **Compliance**: The process to confirm systems compliance with the organization's security standards and policies

Maintainability

Maintainability is the ability of any application to go through modifications and updates with a degree of ease. This is the degree of flexibility with which the application can be modified, whether for bug fixes or to update functionality. These changes may impact any of the components, services, functionality, or interfaces in the application landscape while modifying to fix errors, or to meet changing business requirements.

This is also the degree of time it takes to restore the system to its normal state following a failure or fault. Improving maintainability can improve the availability and reduce the runtime defects. An application's maintainability is dependent on the overall quality attributes.

It is critical as a large chunk of the IT budget is spent on maintenance of systems. The more maintainable a system is, the lower the total cost of ownership.

The following attributes are:

- Conformance to design standards, coding standards, best practices, reference architectures, and frameworks
- Flexibility is the degree to which the system is intended to support change
- Release support is the way in which the system supports the introduction of initial release, phased roll outs, and future releases

Manageability

Manageability is the ease with which the administrators can manage the application, through useful instrumentation exposed for monitoring.

It is the ability of the system, or the group of the system, to provide key information to the operations and support team to be able to debug, analyze, and understand the root cause of failures. It deals with compliance/governance of the domain frameworks and policies.

The key is to design an application that is easy to manage, by exposing useful instrumentation for monitoring systems and for understanding the cause of failures.

The following attributes are:

- System must maintain total traceability of transactions
- Business objects and database fields are part of auditing
- User and transactional timestamps
- File characteristics include size before, size after, and structure
- Getting events and alerts as thresholds (for example, memory, storage, or processor) are breached
- Remotely manage applications and create new virtual instances at the click of a button
- Rich graphical dashboard for all key applications metrics and KPI

Reliability

Reliability is the ability of the application to maintain its integrity and veracity over a time span and also in the event of faults or exceptions. It is measured as the probability that the software will not fail and that it will continue functioning for a defined time interval.

It also specifies the ability of the system to maintain its performance over a time span. Unreliable software is prone to failures and a few processes may be more sensitive to failure than others, because such processes may not be able to recover from a fault or exception.

The following attributes are:

- The characteristic of a system to perform its functions under stated conditions for a specific period of time
- Mean time to recovery; time available to get the system back up online
- Mean time between failures; acceptable threshold for downtime
- Data integrity is also known as referential integrity in database tables and interfaces
- Application integrity and information integrity during transactions
- Fault trapping (I/O), handling failures, and recovery

Extensibility

Extensibility is the ability of a system to cater to future changes through flexible architecture, design, or implementation.

Extensible applications have excellent endurance, which prevents the expensive processes of procuring large inflexible applications and retiering them due to changes in business needs. Extensibility enables organizations to take advantage of opportunities and respond to risks and while there is a significant difference, extensibility is often tangled with modifiability. Modifiability means that it is possible to change the software whereas extensibility means that change has been planned and will be effortless. Adaptability is at times erroneously leveraged with extensibility. However, adaptability deals with how the user interactions with the system are managed and governed.

Extensibility allows a system, people, technology, information, and processes all working together to achieve the following attributes:

- Handle new information types
- Manage new or changed business entities
- Consume or provide new feeds

Recovery

In the event of a natural calamity, for example, a flood or hurricane, the entire facility where the application is hosted may become inoperable or inaccessible. Business-critical applications should have a strategy to recover from such disasters within a reasonable time frame. The solution implementing various processes must be integrated with the existing enterprise disaster recovery plan. The processes must be analysed to understand the criticality of each process to the business, the impact of loss to the business in case of non-availability of the process. Based on this analysis, appropriate disaster procedures must be developed, and plans should be outlined. As part of disaster recovery, electronic backups of data and procedures must be maintained at the recovery location and be retrievable within the appropriate time frames for system function restoration. In the case of high criticality, real-time mirroring to a mirror site should be deployed.

The following attributes are:

- **Recovery process**: **Recovery Time Objectives (RTO)** and **Recovery Point Objectives (RPO)**
- **Restore time**: Time required switching to the secondary site when the primary fails
- **RPO/backup time**: Time it takes to back up your data
- **Backup frequencies**: Frequency of backing up the transaction data, configuration data and code

Interoperability

Interoperability is the ability to exchange information and communicate with internal and external applications and systems.

Interoperable systems make it easier to exchange information both internally and externally. The data formats, transport protocols and interfaces are the key attributes for architecting interoperable systems. Standardization of data formats, transport protocols and interfaces is the key aspect to be considered when architecting an interoperable system.

Interoperability is achieved through:

- Publishing and describing interfaces
- Describing the syntax used to communicate
- Describing the semantics of information it produces and consumes
- Leveraging open standards to communicate with external systems
- Being loosely coupled with external systems

The following attributes are:

- **Compatibility with shared applications**: Other systems it needs to integrate with
- **Compatibility with third party applications**: Other systems it has to live with amicably
- **Compatibility with various OS**: Different OS compatibilities
- **Compatibility on different platforms**: Hardware platforms it needs to work on

Usability

Usability measures characteristics such as consistency and aesthetics in the user interface. Consistency is the constant use of mechanisms employed in the user interface while aesthetics refers to the artistic, visual quality of the user interface.

It is the ease at which the users operate the system and make productive use of it. Usability is discussed with relation to the system interfaces, but it can just as well be applied to any tool, device, or rich system.

This addresses the factors that establish the ability of the software to be understood, used, and learned by its intended users.

The application interfaces must be designed with end users in mind so that they are intuitive to use, are localized, provide access for differently abled users, and provide an excellent overall user experience.

The following attributes are:

- **Look and feel standards**: Layout and flow, screen element density, keyboard shortcuts, UI metaphors, and colours
- **Localization/Internationalization requirements**: Keyboards, paper sizes, languages, spellings, and so on

Summary

This chapter provided the introduction of NFRs and why NFRs are critical for building software systems. The chapter also explained various KPI for each of the key NFRs that is, scalability, availability, reliability, and so on. The book will cover the most critical 24 NFRs that are applicable for IT applications and systems.

The next chapter describes the taxonomy of NFRs that is, scalability, availability, reliability, and so on. The next chapter outlines the entire lifecycle of NFRs and describes a framework that can be leveraged by business analysts and architects for discovering NFRs on engagements. The framework will focus on the KPI and KRA for each of the NFRs which will be the critical input for the solution design phase.

2
Taxonomy and Framework for NFRs

Establishing quality attributes is critical to the success of the applications, as is providing the business functionality. Incorrect customer information can lead to loss and damage to reputation, while poor response time will affect the morale and leads to eventual loss of customers.

Majorly, the approaches to architecture transformation are driven by business or functional requirements. The primary emphasis is on achieving business functionality for the applications or systems. Decisions on achieving functional requirements are done during the architecture or design phases, but for NFRs, they are often not methodical and are undocumented.

At times the quality attributes are often a consequence of other decisions, and done in an unplanned and ad-hoc manner.

The key topics covered in the chapter are as follows:

- Taxonomy and framework
- NFR SDLC

Taxonomy of non-functional requirements

This session describes the software quality attributes that an architect should emphasize while architecting the application.

Refer to the following table to gain a perception of how software quality attributes map to system factors, and the detailed description for each of the software quality attributes.

Later sections of this chapter contain best practice guidelines for each quality attribute, to understand how the attributes will impact the solution design and the dependent decisions to address these issues.

 Remember that the list of quality attributes in this chapter is critical and will be essential to be considered for every application or IT system.

The following table describes all the critical software quality attributes covered in this book. It categorizes the attributes in four categories which includes runtime, design, system, and user. Leverage the following table to understand each of the quality attributes and their associated solution designs:

Category	NFR	Description
Runtime	Performance	Performance is defined as the responsiveness of the application to perform specific actions in a given time span. It is scored in terms of throughput or latency. Latency is the time it takes to respond to an event. Throughput is the number of events clocked in a given time interval.
Runtime	Scalability	Scalability is the ability to handle increase in work load without impacting the performance, or the ability to quickly extend.
Runtime	Availability	Availability is defined as the time span the application is functional normally. It is measured as the percentage of total application downtime over a specified period. Availability is affected by faults and exceptions, infrastructure issues, malicious outbreaks, and maintenance and upgrades.
Design time	Capacity	This non-functional requirement defines the ways in which the system may be expected to scale-up by increasing capacity that is, adding machines based on business growth.

Runtime	Security	Security is the ability of an application to avoid the malicious incidences and events in context of the designed system usage, and prevent loss of information. Improving security would also increase the reliability of application by reducing the likelihood of an attack succeeding and impairing operations.
Design time	Maintainability	Maintainability is the characteristics of the application to go through changes with a degree of ease. The ease with which the application can be modified, whether for bug fixes or to add new functionality. These changes may impact functionality, components, services, or interfaces when modifying the application's functionality to fix errors, or to meet future business needs.
Runtime	Manageability	Manageability is the ease with which the administrators can manage the application landscape, through useful instrumentation revealed through monitoring. This is the ability of the system or the group of the system to provide key information to the operations and support team to be able to debug, analyse and understand the root cause of failures. Manageability deals with compliance with the domain frameworks and policies.
Runtime	Reliability	Reliability is the characteristics of an application to continue running in an expected manner over a span of time. Reliability is usually scored as the probability that the application will not fail and that it will continue functioning for a defined time span.
Design time	Extensibility	Extensibility is a characteristic whereby the architecture, design, and implementation of an application accommodate for future needs. Extensible applications have greater endurance, by avoiding the expensive process of procuring huge inconfigurable applications and then decommissioning them when business needs change.
Runtime	Recovery	Mission-critical systems should have a plan in place to recover from such disasters within a reasonable amount of time.

Runtime	Interoperability	Interoperability is the ability to operate successfully by communicating information and data with both internal and external applications. The interoperable application makes it easier to share information externally and internally.
Design time	Usability	Usability is the characteristics such as aesthetics and consistency in the application UI. Aesthetics is the visual quality of the application UI. Consistency is the constantly leveraging a predefined and tested mechanism for the user interface. Usability is the ease at which the end users operate the applications and make efficient use of the features. Usability is usually discussed in relation to the application UI, but it can as well be applied to a tool, device, or rich system.

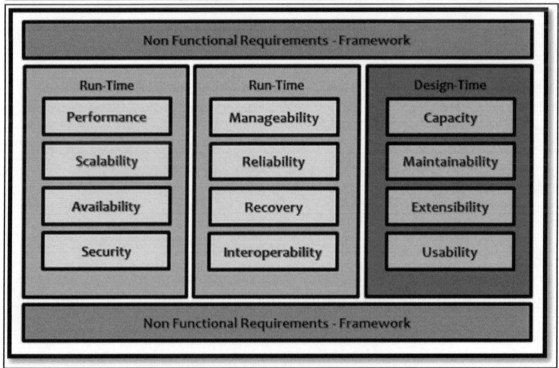

Figure 1: Non-functional requirements

Non-functional requirements framework

In comparison to feature driven approaches, the NFR framework leverages all the key NFRs including security, accuracy, performance and scalability to drive the solution architecture process. The framework puts NFRs foremost on the software architect's agenda.

One has to iterate over the process steps a few times during the design process and finalize the critical NRFs for the engagement. An architect may refine it through various design alternatives and hence the development process may move up and down, rather than being strictly sequential. It will be essential for the architect to draw from past knowledges and experience while working through the process.

The NFR framework provides a model for identifying and establishing the solution design and rationale. The framework also offers a catalogue of NFRs, the sub-NFRs and the decomposing techniques. By drawing on this framework, the knowledge at each checkpoint can be leveraged to initiate and bring forth expertise to drive the NFRs process steps.

NFR life cycle

The five phases of the NFR life cycle discussed later apply to each of the quality dimensions. Developing and maintaining artifacts associated with each of these phases (for each quality dimension) can bring about efficiencies in individual quality life cycles, via application, modification, and re-use of these artifacts.

The NFR life cycle indicates a logical flow (deductive reasoning) from generic (broad objectives) to specific (configuration parameters and specifications) which helps with requirement mapping and tracing.

In general, the activities and inputs/outputs of each phase map to the different architecture disciplines:

- Phase 1 maps to the business architecture as well as the business and IT process architecture, as several of the analytical methods used in Phase 1 are part of a business and IT process, and their outputs can be used as artifacts for the business architecture.
- Phase 2 maps to the business architecture and service architectures that are embedded in the enterprise (and enterprise architecture). There are enterprise-level requirements documents and service-specific requirements documents.
- Phase 3 maps to the IT and IS architecture, primarily in terms of re-use of non-functional requirements building blocks which implement design specifications.

- Phase 4 maps to the **Enterprise (or Event) Monitoring and Management (EMM)** architecture which includes resource, service and business monitoring, and reporting capabilities (associated with functional and non-functional requirements).
- Phase 5 maps to the IT operations architecture, and specifically, data-driven (non-functional requirements-related performance data) **Service Improvement Plans (SIP)** and capabilities.

The following diagram depicts the NFR life cycle:

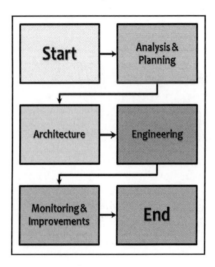

Figure 2: NFR life cycle

Analysis and planning for NFRs

The software architect collates and leverages knowledge about the domain and the system under development. Analysis and planning for non-functional requirements includes leveraging an organization-specific NFR framework and artifacts and initial gathering of non-functional requirements. Certain non-functional requirements can be arrived at via planning and analysis activities. As a case in point, business continuity requirements can be arrived at via business impact analysis, service impact analysis, and risk analysis; all three analytical activities are part of the service continuity management in the ITIL framework. Similarly, cost of service unavailability analysis can help the organization arrive at service availability requirements. These analytical methods that produce requirements documentation are typically part of an IT process and involve business and technology stakeholders.

Artifacts documenting business scenarios and use-case scenarios associated with non-functional requirements can benefit the enterprise from a planning perspective, particularly when these artifacts are re-used and applied when different groups are engaged in documenting non-functional requirements related to the service they are developing or maintaining.

The architect draws on the catalog of NFRs knowledge and design and development techniques. The framework is leveraged to provide a taxonomy and classification of NFR principles and concepts.

The preceding diagram shows the NFRs framework aka catalog. The NFR will be arranged in a hierarchical structure. The NFR KRA and KPI provide a vocabulary to represent requirements. Standard development practices, including the methodology for decomposing NFRs, are also organized in the framework. The framework can be extended to other phases for example, design or development, to deal with additional concepts which can also be addressed.

By leveraging NFR framework, the architect establishes an initial list by identifying the crucial NFRs that the system under development should fulfill. These NFRs are business goals to be delivered and which needs to be analyzed, decomposed, ranked, operationalize. The architect identifies possible development techniques and methodologies. The architect will choose options for target state that will meet the business requirements. Thus the architect begins by thoroughly disintegrating the initial NFR into sub-goals.

The following NFR framework steps are leveraged for analysis of requirements, followed by architecture and design stages:

- First, the business goals are broken down into smaller goals. The ambiguities are resolved and domain information and priorities and leveraged.
- Next, the architect creates solutions to build quality into the system under development, SuD.
- Thirdly, all alternatives and options are considered for the target system, then the best option is finalized and design decisions are established.
- Finally, an analysis is done to check if deviation from stated NFRs is made.

The architect may choose to decompose the NFRs by topic or type. To efficiently tackle with such a broad set of requirements, the NFR may be broken down into smaller goals, so that the solution architecture can be defined. There may be times that the requirements are ambiguous. There may be different concepts of security controls in the context of customer bank information. Treating this high-level requirement will need decomposing it into more specific sub-goals which together satisfice end objective of the NFRs. All the several sub-goals will be required together to meet a final goal. For example, if confidentiality, integrity, and availability are met, then the overall contribution will be achieving the security NFR.

Architecture for NFR

Architecture for non-functional requirements refines all of the non-functional requirements to develop architecture specifications. Architecture specifications and domain architecture specifications, are some of the key outputs of this phase.

Non-functional requirements-related use-case scenarios and use-cases are also key outputs of this phase. Mapping of non-functional requirements to standards are also part of this phase. Domains include application, data, and **integration system (IS)** domains as well as network, server, storage, facilities, systems management, desktop, and other such technology domains. Architecture for non-functional requirements covers the process of evaluation and selection of a set of design patterns and building blocks that have the potential to implement a sets of non-functional requirements. Architecting for non-functional requirements also includes the process of refining non-functional requirements and mapping of non-functional requirements to specific architecture building blocks.

Engineering for NFRs

Design, build, and test specifications are key outputs of this phase. These specifications can be service-specific or at the domain level. Test case scenarios and test cases are also important outputs of this phase which helps with the traceability of the non-functional requirements from gathering to realization. Non-functional requirements engineering, design, and build as well as testing help with the implementation of solutions that meet or exceed non-functional requirements. Non-functional requirements engineering includes:

- Non-functional requirements engineering, such as performance engineering
- Design for non-functional requirements, such as designing for availability
- Building with non-functional requirements building blocks
- Testing for each non-functional requirements test case

Standards-related specifications are a key part of this phase and the next phase. Several standards organizations provide documented specifications that are very relevant for re-use during the engineering and operating phases of the NFR life cycle.

When the NFRs are adequately refined, software architect will be able to identify possible solution for architecting these NFRs for the target state. The development techniques are the methodology for arriving at the target state. However, there may be a gap between NFR goals and solution methodology and one must bridge the gap to get to the destination. This involves extensive analysis and handling various factors. These include priorities, ambiguities, tradeoffs, and domain information including the workload of the organization. These factors will have to be addressed in the entire process chain.

An alternative to providing optimum response time is to leverage indexing. Indexing is a database design methodology for optimum response times. Indexing will helps meet the NFR goals for response time. Also leveraging uncompressed format will make a positive influence on establishing the response time. Indexing or uncompressed format are the best alternatives for achieving good response times.

Framework will aid the search and solutioning of NFRs. The progression from NFR goals to solutioning is a key step in the design process because NFRs needs to be converted into implementable entities. However, it may not be possible to convert initial requirements into a concrete solution definition in one step. There will be iterative refinements and expansions steps. Furthermore, software architect needs to carry-on identifying development techniques alternative and finalize them.

We need to emphasize on meeting the NFRs goals priority. Priorities may come up from attention of several factors. These include domains such as priorities and load capacity. In addition, requirements may be identified as priorities during different development steps. Few priorities will be designated as critical, as they are the key to the success of the business or organization goals. Others will be defined as prevailing, as they form a significant portion of the organization's workload.

After identifying the priorities, it will be analyzed and operationalized. For example, priorities may be leveraged to decide appropriate tradeoffs for NFR business goals. Information about the tradeoffs is documented, and made available for dealing with conflicts and collaboration. Thus throughout the development methodology, different tradeoffs considerations are made and rationales established.

During the analysis and solutioning process, choices are made to achieve a particular NFR, it is highly possible that some other NFR gets affected, either positively or negatively. These interactions are critical because they have a bearing on the decision process for achieving the overall NFRs. They may either have negative or positive impacts but will be managed in a variety of ways and documented in the design specifications.

An essential technique about the framework is that design decisions must be supported by well-justified rationale or decisions. Rationale will be established for making refinement or choosing an option. The solution process will continue till various options for the target state are sufficiently established, and no other options are conceivable. During the entire process, the architect will review the NFRs, domain, and will address ambiguities and trade-offs.

The architect then considers possible solution definition, design rationale, and dependencies, using knowledge from the past. Early decisions may need to be taken into account when making decisions. This information is documented and is available to help the architect decide among the alternatives. The architect will drive the decision making to finally arrive at the target system architecture. In order to produce a target state, the architect has to choose from the possible operationalizations or options. Additionally, correct design rationale should be determined and documented. There will be various choices for operationalizing NFR goals of those identified alternatives; some are chosen, while the others will be rejected.

All the architecture and design decisions are considered to establish the impact. The evaluation of design decisions emphasizes the fact that a chosen option is good for the target architecture. This methodology of reasoning will be correct for dealing with NFRs as meeting these NFRs is often a matter of degree.

Monitoring and improvements - NFRs

Each non-functional requirement has a set of sub-qualities and metrics that are associated with each sub-quality. How does the service in question perform against the service quality targets set for the service? This question can be answered with the **Enterprise Monitoring and Management (EMM)** architecture and capabilities. EMM tools can help with business, service, and resource monitoring and reporting. Measurable and reportable metrics that map to the non-functional requirements are key for non-functional requirements monitoring. SMART metrics are Specific, Measurable, Achievable, Relevant, and Time-bound.

Non-functional requirements themselves can be performance targets for certain key metrics. For example, **Mean Time to Restore Service (MTTRS)** is a key metric for availability and recoverability (sub-quality), and number and percent of time the 30 minutes MTTRS is met or exceeded for email as a service becomes a measurable and reportable non-functional requirement metric for e-mail.

Metrics models such as the **Distributed Management Task Force (DMTF)** CIM metrics model with its **Unit of Work (UoW)** definition, base metric definition, and base metric value provide a standards-based model for defining and managing non-functional requirements-related metrics.

As per the CIM metrics model, there can be several units of work such as batch jobs, user-initiated interactive operations, completed and committed transactions, and so on associated with a service. There are also several metrics associated with each UoW.

UoW metrics and measurements are at a more granular level than service metrics. A UoW can have several associated non-functional requirements metrics, even though the CIM metrics model-related UoW metrics are primarily time taken to complete the UoW (performance dimension) and status of the UoW (availability dimension).

In ITIL parlance, **Continuous Service Improvement (CSI)** and **Service Improvement Plans (SIP)** involve measures to improve service qualities and service capability to meet or exceed non-functional requirements.

For example, service outage analysis and the application availability patterns result in availability improvement plans, particularly when IT organizations face **Service Level Agreement (SLA)** breaches due to unplanned outages.

Similarly, IT organizations can have improvement plans for each service quality or sub-quality discussed in this White Paper.

New and emerging technologies, processes, and organizational capabilities can directly improve certain service qualities.

Examples include replication technologies and the exponential decline in the cost of storage space (disk space measured in gigabytes), which has allowed for significant improvements in service continuity capabilities.

Another example is grid storage that offers improved storage performance and resilience capabilities over older storage methods. The NFR life cycle results in the realization and improvement of a service performance when it comes to non-functional requirements. The following table describes NFR framework:

NFR	Attributes
Performance	• Throughput: The ability of the system to execute a given number of transactions within a given unit of time • Response times: The allowable distribution of time which the system takes to respond to request
Scalability	• Throughput: Number of maximum transactions your system needs to handle, for example, thousand a day or A million • Storage: Amount of data you going to need to store • Growth requirements: Data growth in the next 3-5 years
Availability (uptime)	• Availability: Application availability considering the weekends, holidays and maintenance times and failures • Locations of operation: Geographic location, Connection requirements and the restrictions of a local network prevail • Offline requirement: Time available for offline operations including batch processing and system maintenance • Length of time between failures • Recoverability: Time required by the system is able to resume operation in the event of failure • Resilience: The reliability characteristics of the system and sub-components • MTBF : Length of time between failures • MTTR : Length of time needed to resume operation after a failure • Availability = MTBF/(MTBF+MTTR)
Capacity (provisioning for growth)	• Throughput: Number of peak transactions the system needs to handle • Storage: Volume of data the system will page/persist at runtime to disk. This relates to the memory/disk • Year-on-year growth requirements (users, processing and storage) • e-channel growth projections • Activities or transactions supported for each type of transaction, volumes on an hourly, daily, weekly, monthly and so on • Volumes are significantly higher during specific parts of the day (for example, at lunch), week, month or year • Transaction volume growth expected and additional volumes you will be able to handle

Security (define key security requirements)	• Authentication: Correct identification of parties attempting to access systems and protection of systems from unauthorized parties
	• Authorization: Mechanism required to authorize users to perform different functions within the systems
	• Encryption (data in flight and at rest): All external communications between the system's data server and clients must be encrypted
	• Data confidentiality: All data must be protectively marked, stored and protected
	• Compliance: The process to confirm systems compliance with the organizations security standards and policies:
	  ○ Resistance to known attacks (to be enumerated)
	  ○ Time/efforts/resources needed to find a key (probability of finding the key)
	  ○ Probability/time/resources to detect an attack
	  ○ Percentage of useful services still available during an attack
	  ○ Percentage of successful attacks
	  ○ Lifespan of a password, of a session

Maintainability (the ease with which the system can be maintained)	• Conformance to design standards, coding standards, best practices, reference architectures and framework
	• Flexibility: The degree to which the system is intended to support change
	• Release Support: The way in which the system will support the introduction of initial release, phased rollouts and future releases:
	  ○ Coupling/cohesion metrics
	  ○ Number of anti-patterns
	  ○ Cyclomatic complexity
	  ○ Mean time to fix a defect
	  ○ Mean time to add new functionality
	  ○ Quality and quantity of documentation

Manageability	• System must maintain full traceability of transactions • Audited objects and audited database fields to be included for auditing • File characteristics: size before, size after, structure • User and transactional time stamps, and so on • Get notices and alerts as thresholds (for example, storage, memory, processor) are approached • Remotely manage systems and create new virtual instances at the 'click of a button' • Rich graphical dashboard for all key applications metrics
Reliability	• The ability of a system to perform its required functions under stated conditions for a specific period of time • Mean Time Between Failures: Acceptable threshold for down-time • Mean Time To Recovery: Time is available to get the system back up online • Data integrity: Referential integrity in database tables and interfaces • Application integrity and information integrity: During transactions • Fault trapping (I/O): Handling failures and recovery • Defect rate • Degree of precision of computation
Extensibility	• Handle new information types • Manage new or changed business entities • Consume or provide new feeds
Recovery (in the event of failure)	• Recovery process: Recovery Point Objectives (RPO) and Recovery Time Objectives (RTO) • RTO/Restore time: Time required to switch to secondary site when the primary fails • RPO/Backup time: Time taken to back your data • Backup frequencies: Frequency of backing-up the transaction data, config data and code

Interoperability	• Compatibility with shared applications: Other systems it need to integrate • Compatibility with third party applications: Other systems it has to live with amicably • Compatibility on different operating systems: Different OS compatibility • Compatibility on different platforms: Hardware platforms it needs to work on
Usability	• Look and feel standards--screen element density, layout and flow, colours, UI metaphors, keyboard shortcuts • Internationalization / localization requirements-- languages, spellings, keyboards, paper sizes, and so on • Proportion of functionalities or tasks mastered after a given training time • Acceptable response time • Number of tasks performed or problems resolved in a given time • Number of mouse clicks needed to get to information or functionality • Number (or ratio) of learned tasks that can still be performed after not using the system for a given time period • Number of error per time period and user class • Number of calls to user support • Mean time to recover from an error and be able to continue the task • Satisfaction ratio per user class and usage ratio

NFRs KPI and KRA examples

The next section lists KPI and KRA examples for all the critical NFRs.

Performance

Please check the following table on performance for more details:

NFR attribute	Target value
Transaction processing time (read/write)	1 second
Transaction processing time for complex transaction	5 seconds

Total number of users (registered)	100,000 customers
Average length of user session	5 minutes
Query processing time (read only)	1 second
Batch processing time	5 minutes

Scalability

Please check the following table on scalability for more details:

NFR attribute	Target value
Ability to scale up to *n* users in a year (read only)	500,000 users
Ability to scale up to *n* users in a year (transactions)	100, 000 users
Number of concurrent users during peak periods	4000 users
Session duration	Average 12 minutes
Query processing time (read only)	1 second
Response time for search	5 seconds

Availability

Please check the following table on availability for more details:

NFR attribute	Target value
Time required for the system to become available in normal recovery mode	O minute
Geographies and time zones that impact the systems	None
Availability requirements for different geographies	None
Frequency of scheduled planned outage activity that is acceptable	Monthly
When should be mission critical system be available for the users	99.5 % (24*7)
When should be non-mission critical system be available for the users	98.3
Elapsed time acceptable for service to recover from incident	Days, hours, minutes

Capacity

Please check the following table on capacity for more details:

NFR attribute	Target value
Maximum number of concurrent sessions	4000
Maximum number of concurrent transaction	2000
Expected number of transaction for batch processing	None
Expected number of concurrent users	5000
Expected number of peak users	5000
Number of records (active and archive)	1 million yearly
Ability to store and retrieve business data	7 years

Security

Please check the following table on security for more details:

NFR attribute	Target value
Authorization and authentication	Ability to apply access controls and privileges based access to specific areas Authentication for internal systems should be against the internal LDAP database Every authentication attempt must be logged
Encryption	All private or sensitive information is transmitted using strong encryption and authentication 128 bit or better encryption for SSL/https 3-DES or better encryption for VPN connections No private data stored on Internet accessible machines
Access and control	Authorization for internal systems should be centralised into an LDAP database
Auditing	Include all authentication and authorization events will have detailed audit logs The transaction will have a detailed audit log Inquiries will have a detailed audit log

Maintainability

Please check the following table on maintainability for more details:

NFR attribute	Target value
List of active users subscribed should be maintained by the administrator	Yes
Functionalities to be maintaining at customer level	Yes
Ability for error messages to be customisable by an administrator	Yes

Manageability

Please check the following table on manageability for more details:

NFR attribute	Target value
Alerts required when the system suffers from a recoverable interruption	Yes
Alerts required with the system does not complete its overnight processing in the allotted time frame	Yes
The key data that needs to be captured to measure the performance of the system against the SLAs	Yes
Logging and tracking	Includes all authentication and authorization events The transaction will have a detailed audit Inquiries will have a detailed audit Ability to log user activity and access/recall based on privileges; that is, registration, authentication, product, content, third party

Reliability

Please check the following table on reliability for more details:

NFR attribute	Target value
Mean Time Between Failures --acceptable threshold for down-time	100000 Hrs

Mean Time To Recovery--time available to get the application back online	10 Hrs
Data integrity	Dependent data not to be impacted by uncommitted data (Consistent, Atomic) Long running transactions not to impact read processes (Isolated) Committed transactions to survive system crashes or downtime (Durable)
Application integrity	Application rollbacks to keep the data consistent. Ability to access system from external environments via secure web interfaces; based on privilege access controls

Extensibility

Please check the following table on extensibility for more details:

NFR attribute	Target value
Extensibility options	The logical separation of the application into different tiers (client, presentation, business logic, integration and EIS tier) allows a system to be flexible and easily maintainable Leveraging design patterns throughout the application architecture. Object orientation like encapsulation, inheritance, low coupling and high cohesion are leveraged in application design Is supported by proper documentation of the application Independence of interface from implementation

Recovery

Please check the following table on recovery for more details:

NFR attribute	Target value
Recovery Point Objectives (RPO)/Restore time	2 Days
Recovery Time Objectives (RTO)/Backup time	Every 4 hours

Interoperability

Please check the following table on interoperability for more details:

NFR attribute	Target value
Interoperability options	Ability to communicate to internal and external systems through recognised and accepted protocols. These protocols include SOAP, HTTP, FTP, and XML. Ability to communicate to other internal and external systems through known mechanisms. These include SOA and Event-Driven mechanisms. Export of information to be available in approved formats and standards. These standards include CSV and XML. Ability to comply with the **W3C Web Content Accessibility Guidelines (WCAG)**.

Usability

Please check the following table on usability for more details:

NFR attribute	Target value
Usability options	Ability for an interface design that minimises the need for manual keying for example, information already contained in system tables which would result in relevant drop-down lists rather than having to key Ability to enable the use of the computer's operational settings (for example, local, regional and resolution settings) in the browser Ability to support the different browsers: Internet Explorer, Chrome, Mozilla Firefox, Safari, Netscape Ability to support the following screen resolutions for PC's: (1024x768, 800x600, 1280 x 1024, 1280x800, 1152x864) Ability to support the following delivery mediums: PC, mobile phones, PDA

Is anything different from the standard NCB usability features required	Yes
Are there users with special needs	No
What level of system help will be required?	Detailed
What will determine the application language to be displayed ?	User selection

Summary

The chapter described the taxonomy of NFRs that is, scalability, availability, reliability and so on. The chapter outlined the entire life cycle of NFRs, The chapter described a framework that can leveraged by business analyst and architects for discovering NFRs on various engagements. The framework will focus on the KPIs and KRA for each of the NFRs which will be the critical input for the solution design phase.

The next chapter outlines methodology for discovering (elicitations) NFRs. The chapter will describe a framework that can be leveraged by business analyst for elicitations of NFRs. The chapter will outlines framework for prioritization of NFRs. The output of this stage will be the critical input for the solution architecture phase.

3
Methodology Eliciting - Non Functional Requirements

Critical success factors for business initiatives are the creation of precise functional requirements, defining the behavior of the system, and NFRs, which describe how the system will accomplish its goals. The business stakeholders may define functional requirements well, but be challenged when it comes to non-functional requirements. If you ask the business stakeholders the right questions, you should be able to achieve a better alignment between business and IT.

In software development, the gathering of requirements is the first step. Functional requirements describe the behaviors of the application that support the business goals, and NFRs include constraints and qualities. Just as with tracking the functional requirements to closure during the different phases of software development, it is imperative for the success of any IT engagement to elicit, document, and track NFRs from the beginning through to closure.

The key topics covered in this chapter are as follows:

- Elicitations and discovery
- NFR prioritization and cost benefit analysis
- Analysis, KPIs and metrics and NFR SDLC

NFRs have a life cycle which starts with the requirements definition, moves to the solution design and implementation, and finishes with quality assurance. The NFR life cycle phases mentioned later in this chapter will apply to each software quality attribute. Creating artefacts for NFRs will bring efficiencies to the software life cycle, via leveraging best practices, standards and re-use. The NFR life cycle defines a proper flow from generic goals to specific attributes that will help in requirements charting and traceability.

Methodology discovering non-functional requirements

Business scenarios will be the key outcome of the analysis phase related to NFRs. These business scenarios may have interlinked user scenarios.

As an example, numerous business scenarios will be interlinked with the business continuity processes. Similar outcomes will be associated for scenarios with regard to availability events. The user scenario analysis will become complex with the sourcing of applications. However, specifications for business scenarios related to NFRs can benefit the organization from a planning and strategy perspective, specifically when these specifications are leveraged by different teams engaged in documenting NFRs, and in developing and maintaining business entities.

Non-functional requirements scenarios, which includes user stories, business scenarios, and so on, are the key output of this phase. The charting of NFRs to standards and best practices is also part of the life cycle. Architecting non-functional requirements includes the selection of design patterns and architecture building blocks that will implement the specific non-functional requirements. It also consists of refining and decomposing NFRs, as well as mapping NFRs to specific technology building blocks.

There are different processes and methodologies for elucidating non-functional requirements. The NFR framework will provide a guideline to the NFRs as well as the KPI; but as the next steps, the business analyst will have to leverage a combination of methods. This will include a top-down and bottom-up approach to tackling NFRs.

Best practices for discovering NFRs include stakeholder goals, concerns, current state analysis, market analysis, and domain trends, among other things.

The following sections describe these in further detail.

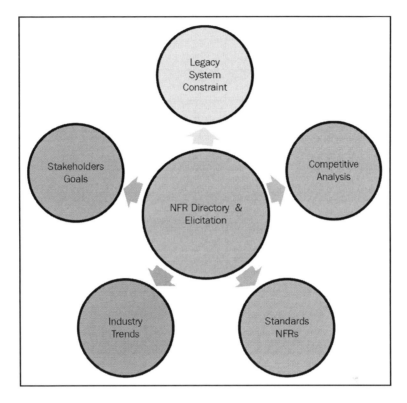

Figure 1: NFR elicitation

Stakeholder goals

Workshops and discussions held with stakeholders from the business and technology groups are one of the key steps in this process. The business analyst must identify the key KPIs for the business stakeholders. The software qualities, that attributes must attain in order to achieve business objectives, must address the stakeholder's challenge, issues and concerns.

For example, the application should be able to generate a new transaction every 10 minutes otherwise the end users will consider the new application is too slow.

Legacy system restraints

The business analyst analyzes constraints dictated by the runtime environment in which the new application should run, the existing applications it must integrate, and the platform infrastructure it must leverge.

Service Improvement Plan (SIP) and **Continuous Service Improvement (CSI)** consist of procedures to improvise service capabilities and qualities to meet NFRs.

For example, application availability patterns and service outage analysis will result in availability improvisation plans, specifically when enterprises are facing service level agreement breaches due to outages. Similarly, enterprises may have an improvement plan for each service software qualities.

Market scan of software qualities

Additional NFRs can be identified by analysing the software qualities of competitor applications. For example, the number of users with which the competitor application can support, and the need to scale it up or down.

Domain trends

Emerging processes and technologies can directly impact service software qualities. For example, it includes:

- Replication technologies and the decline in the cost of storage component space, and has allowed substantial improvements in service continuity ability.
- Grid storage that provides resilience capabilities and improved performance over older storage processes and methods.
- Analyzing the roadmap the vertical industry is taking and then identifying key NFR trends. This also requires articulating and leveraging best practices, standards and reference frameworks. For example, do customers expect faster response times or average growth interms of number of transactions in the vertical industry.

Requirements templates and catalogues

A business analyst typically leverages best practice templates, frameworks, and catalogues during this phase. Questions will be asked about each type of non-functional requirement and are done using a questionnaire for NFRs; for example, usability, scalability, performance, availability, stability, extensibility, and so on.

The NFR life cycle processes results in the improvement of a service performance for non-functional requirements. Standards and best practice specifications are a key part of these phases. Standards bodies provide documented best practice artifacts that can be re-used for various phases of the NFR life cycle.

Architecting non-functional requirements consists of the evaluation and selection of a set of architecture building blocks and technology patterns that will implement specific non-functional requirements. This process also includes refining and decomposing (slicing and dicing) non-functional requirements and mapping non-functional requirements to technology building blocks.

Each non-functional requirement will have sub-qualities and metrics associated with each sub-quality. The performance of software quality against the quality targets is monitored and analyzed through the **Enterprise Monitoring and Management (EMM)** capabilities.

EMM is also known as **application performance management (APM)** and is discussed later in this book. EMM tools provide support for business monitoring and reporting. Measurable metrics for the service qualities or NFRs are key for non-functional requirements monitoring.

Non-functional requirements may be performance targets for organizational metrics. For example, **Mean Time to Restore Service (MTTRS)** is a key metric for service availability and recoverability. For example, the percent of time the 30 minutes MTTRS is met or exceeded for e-mail becomes a measurable non-functional requirement metric for e-mail services.

Several organizations treat availability, continuity, and security as the most critical non-functional requirements, and classify them as such. The remaining non-functional requirements dimensions are important but treated as secondary when compared to availability, continuity, and security. The prioritization scheme may vary from one industry to another and one organization to another.

As a case in point, an online brokerage firm competing on the basis of cost and value to its customer can treat service efficiency, especially from a cost structure perspective, as critical to the firm's strategy and competitive advantage. As such, efficiency becomes a key non-functional requirements dimension both for domain architectures and service architectures. In fact, the online brokerage firm's IT department has a dedicated and collaborative process to constantly look for cost-cutting opportunities and to implement them faster than its competition. This enterprise was among the first in the industry to replace several of its high-end UNIX systems with low-end Linux systems in the 1990s. The penetration of low-cost Linux systems in the firm's data centers is also the in the industry. An enterprise's business and IT strategy, business model, and industry and regulatory environments are some of the factors that determine the prioritization scheme.

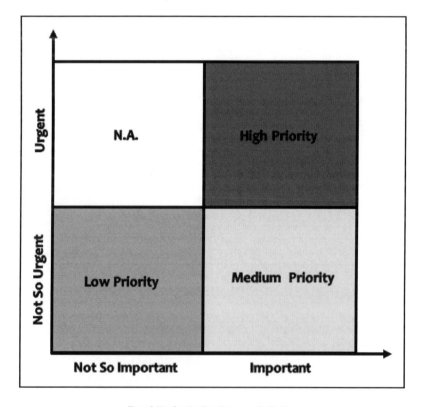

Figure 2: Non-functional requirements - prioritization

Summary

This chapter outlined the methodology for discovering (elicitating) NFRs. It described a framework that can be leveraged by business analysts/solution architects/SMEs for elicitations of NFRs. The chapter also outlined a framework for prioritization of NFRs. The output of this stage will be the critical input for the solution architecture phase.

The next chapter outlines the solution part of NFRs, providing insights, guidance and principles for architecting NFRs. It covers all the key NFRs that are critical for any project; and, for each NFR, it provides the various alternatives pertaining to the solution and the design principles that need to be applied to achieve the desired outcome; for example, high availability, or scalability, or reliability, and so on. The chapter includes considerations for bespoke (Java, .NET) and COTS applications and are applicable for any IT applications/systems in different domains.

4
Solutions Addressing NFRs

NFRs are the software quality attributes that impact runtime functions, software architecture, and customer experience. NFRs have the potential for application-wide impact across tiers and layers. Some NFRs are related to the design time attributes, while others are specific to runtime, or customer focus. The degree to which the architecture displays amalgamation of software quality attributes, such as scalability or capacity, indicates the success of the architecture and the quality of the overall solution.

When architecting solutions to meet the software quality attributes, it is essential to consider the impact on other NFRs as well. An architect has to analyze the trade-offs between different NFRs as they are interlinked or interdependent. The criticality of each NFR differs from application to application; for example, interoperability will be less critical in a single **common off-the-shelf** (**COTS**) application for the retail domain than in a business critical system.

The key topics covered in this chapter are as follows:

- Architecting non-functional requirements and techniques related to architecture of NFRs
- Understanding various tools, techniques, methodologies, and enterprise topologies
- Best practice architecting, metrics, KPIs and checklist for NFRs
- Concepts, principles, and guidelines for various NFRs
- Methodology for architecting NFRs

NFR modeling methodology

Let's see each of the methologies in detail.

Performance

Performance is defined as the responsiveness of the application to perform specific tasks in a given span of time. It is scored in terms of throughput or latency. Throughput is the number of events in a given span of time while latency is the time it takes to respond to an incident. An application's performance directly impacts software scalability. Enhancing an application's performance often enhances scalability by virtue of reducing shared resource contention.

Performance attributes specify the timing features of the application. There will be a few features that will be more time-sensitive than others. The NFRs should mark the functions that have constraints on their performance. For example, response time relates to the times used to complete specific business processes, batch or interactive, within the target business system. The application must be architected to meet the agreed response time requirements, while supporting the organizational workload.

Key drivers

The following lists:

- Reduced throughput, increased response time, and over utilization server resource
- Increase in consumption of memory, resulting in performance deterioration and an inability to find the required data in the cache, resulting in increased database access
- Increase in database server processing, resulting in reduced throughput
- Failure to architect effective and optimum database processing may overload the database tier
- Inability to meet organization performance goals and an increase in costs
- The increase in network bandwidth use, resulting in delayed response times and an increase in client and server workload

Methodology

This process involves the following key aspects:

Step 1:

Identify and prioritize business use scenarios and applicable performance scenarios, which should be mapped to each of the business-critical processes.

The scenarios should be compiled based on interviews with the business and by analyzing historical data. Next, the scenarios should be prioritized based upon their importance and occurrence probabilities. Each of these scenarios should be mapped to a design principle that should be implemented.

For example, in an e-commerce application, the shopping cart steps and checkout process are the most critical scenarios, and they directly contribute to revenues. Product recommendations, search experience, and personalization scenarios provide an indirect contribution to revenue.

Step 2:

Model the load for each of the business scenarios identified in the previous step, and identify the potential workload. The workload could be one of the following:

- Total number of users (anonymous and registered) and the average think time
- Number of concurrent users
- Number of page visits
- Number of transactions per hour
- The volume of input and output data

Response time objectives are substantial in the context of a defined organizational workload. It may be easier for an application to process a transaction in six seconds, but difficult to realize this goal when receiving 1,000 transactions per second. This means that the requirement needs to specify the context of a specified goal, consisting of when a transaction begins and when it finishes. In many applications, response time under a fixed load will vary according to the distribution curve. Most transactions will complete close to the average response time mark, but some will take longer, and a few will take less time. Usually, it's unreasonable to expect all transactions to complete within a target response time. It is more realistic to assume a proportion, such as 80- 90%, to meet these objectives.

Throughput is defined in terms of transactions per second, or minute, or hour, where a transaction is a measurable unit of work. The transactions leveraged for throughput planning should typically be established from the application's primary business scenarios. Workload forms a critical input in designing the enterprise application and the infrastructure. Use surveys, historical analysis of the existing systems, and a business roadmap all provide input to the workflow modeling process.

Step 3:

Identify performance-related patterns after determining the key scenarios, and model the workload for each of them.

The following are a few instances of patterns, similar trends related to locations, access devices, and demographics should be analyzed. This helps in accurate performance modeling and testing. This modeling contributes to quantify the performance expectations and helps in accurately design.

Solution options

The solution options are as follows:

- The efficiency and effectiveness of a performance strategy are closely tied to a caching strategy. From a performance standpoint, having an efficient and elaborate caching mechanism is the first step in the process. Take the inventory of all key application components and come up with a strategy to cache the data that will speed up the overall process.
- Evaluate all possibilities of failure and their likely probability. A few common failure events could be hardware failure, security breaches, natural disasters, a sudden spike in traffic, network failure, and so on. For each of these events, attach a weight and probability of its occurrence. Then devise a fault-tolerance mechanism for each of these events. The fault handling procedures and failover options minimize the latency issues caused by failed components.
- Design solutions so that they can be distributed across multiple nodes. This offers a dual advantage of both performance and scalability.
- The key components should be kept lightweight by minimizing their overall size and minimizing server round trips. The most popular way of implementing a lightweight design is to use asynchronous JavaScript and XML - AJAX-based components with no or minimum JavaScripting. This reduces the impact on page size as well as the number of page refreshes and server round-trips.
- Leverage the AJAX-based approach, whether it be for client-side components, communicating with the server, or for data aggregation,. Non-blocking loads using asynchronous data requests drastically improve the perceived page load time and provides a non-blocking loading of the page.
- While retrieving data from systems, such as a database or web services, it is recommended to batch the requests to reduce server round-trips. Most of the database APIs and **object-relational mapping (ORM)** frameworks provide batching functionality.
- Leveraging open standards not only allows for future painless extension of the technology stack, but it also helps in understanding the technology and troubleshooting in the case of performance issues.

- Software components should be loosely coupled so that the failure of a performance issue with one component does not impact the overall response time.
- Adopt continuous code build, deployment, and testing to discover performance issues early in the SDLC. Often, performance testing is done during the end phases of the project, which is expensive and complex to troubleshoot.
- The various tiers should be hosted on different hardware machines. Resource intensive operations and the database are deployed on dedicated hardware, providing improved performance.
- Leverage resource pooling in the application container to improve the performance. Use of connection pooling for database connections will improve performance.
- Load balancing is a key technique to spread the load evenly between various nodes. Load balancing or distribution through the Round Robin DNS algorithm will facilitate in superior performance.
- Lower traffic on the wire by sending only what is required and retrieving only what is necessary.
- Reduce the number of transitions between boundaries, and reduce the amount of data transferred over the wire. Choose batch mode to minimize calls over the network channel.
- Where communication tier boundaries are crossed, leverage coarse-grained interfaces requiring a reduced number of calls for a specific process, and consider using an asynchronous model of communication.
- Design effective locking, transaction, queuing, and threading mechanisms. Leverage optimum queries for superior performance, and avoid bulk data fetching when only a subset is required for the operation. Leverage asynchronous APIs, message queuing, or one-way calls to minimize blocking while making calls across tier boundaries.
- Application, database, and server tuning will also improve system performance.
- Architect efficient communication methodology and protocols between tiers to ensure entities securely interact with no performance degradation.
- Leverage container built-in features, such as distributed transaction and authentication, that will improve robustness and simplify architecture.
- Largely granular interfaces require multiple invocation to perform a task and are the best solution alternatives when located on the same physical node.
- Interfaces that make only one call to accomplish each task provide outstanding performance when the components are distributed across physical boundaries.

- Separate long-running critical processes that might fail by using a separate physical cluster. For example, a web server provides superior processing capacity and memory, but may not have robust storage that can be swapped rapidly in the event of a hardware failure.

Checklist

The checklist for the capture of requirements is as follows:

- Are performances targets identified and approved by the principal stakeholders?
- Are targets for both throughput and response time identified?
- Do the targets differentiate between observed performance and actual performance?
- Have you assessed performance targets rationally?
- Are all performance targets within the context of a workload identified?
- Is there a model to determine the expected performance of the elements that combine to produce the organizational performance dashboards?
- Is there a method to collect instrumentation and management information on actual performance and to compare it to the organization's performance targets? Is the data collated sufficient to identify the elements causing performance bottlenecks?
- Are the expectations of stakeholders set as to what is feasible in your architecture?
- Can you generate a search and display, including text and graphics, for a full web-page within n seconds on an X00 MBs backbone?
- Can you make a listing available to a destination channel within n seconds of storing the listing request?

The checklist for architecture definition is as follows:

- Are performance-related assumptions identified and validated?
- Is the architecture reviewed and assessed for common performance pitfalls and issues?
- Is enough testing and analysis performed to understand the likely performance capabilities of the application?
- Are the potential performance issues in the architecture identified?
- Do you know the extent the proposed architecture can scale without major changes?

- Do you know which load the application can handle? Are different workloads prioritized?

KPIs

The KPI's are stated as follows:

- Throughput: The ability of the system to execute a specified number of transactions in a given timespan
- Response times: The allowable distribution of time which the system takes to respond to the request
- Time it takes to complete a transaction

Scalability

Scalability is the ability of the application to handle an increase in workload without performance degradion, or its ability to quickly enlarge. It is the ability to enlarge the architecture to accommodate more users, more processes, more transactions, and additional nodes and services as the business requirements change and as the system evolves to meet the future needs of the business. The existing systems are extended as far as possible without replacing them. Scalability directly affects the architecture as well as the selection of hardware and system software components.

The solution must allow the hardware and the deployed software services and components to be scaled horizontally as well as vertically. Horizontal scaling involves replicating the same functionality across additional nodes; vertical scaling involves the same functionality across bigger and more powerful nodes. Scalability definitions measure volumes of users and data the system should support.

Key drivers

The key drivers are as follows:

- Applications are unable to handle the increase in workload.
- End users are incurring delays in response times.
- The application is unable to queue requests and process it during reduced load phases.
- Non-distribuable computation or resource: Any computation or a resource, if not distributed, is highly likely to cause a bottleneck scenario.

- For instance, a single server node is an example of a resource that is not distributed.
- High resource-consuming component or computation: Any computation or a software component that consumes massive resources, such as CPU, memory, or network under normal workload, could potentially become a bottleneck.

Methodology

This process involves the following key aspects:

Scalability requirements are defined in terms of an increase in user-load that the system must be able to absorb while continuing to meet its response time and throughput objectives. Scalability requirements also include the changes to the application needed to meet these increased load levels.

The main factors that should be addressed during scalability design are as follows:

- Business SLAs, which include the page response times, transaction and process completion time, initial load times, and others
- Website traffic and workload, which include the average and a maximum number of users, maximum load, maximum number of **transactions per second (TPS)**
- Historical data about seasonal trends is relevant for retail domain-based applications
- The maximum user load supported by competitors and the generally accepted industry standards for response times

Solution options

The solution options are as follow:

- There are two architecture choices for achieving scalability: vertically, by adding additional memory, processors or disks; and horizontally, by adding more machines to the system. Vertical scalability is easier to achieve than horizontal scalability.
- Handling more customer requests requires the system to be scaled by deploying additional web servers.
- Design layers and tiers for scalability, that is, to scale out or scale up a web, application, or database tier.

- The key scalability patterns include distributed computing, parallel computing, SOA, event-driven architecture, push-and-pull data modeling, optimal load sharing, enterprise portals, and message modeling.
- Clustering allows the ability to add processing capability by simply adding nodes to the cluster.
- Use connection pooling for database and resource pooling improves the scalability of applications. Resource pooling, such as database connection pools, is for maintaining multiple logical connections over fewer physical connections and then reusing the connections, bringing in more scalable efficiencies.
- Supplementary application or database servers can be added (horizontal scaling) to improve the scalability of the application.
- Partition data across multiple database servers to improve scalability and allowing flexible location for data sets.
- Design logical layers on the same physical tier to reduce the number of physical nodes while also increasing load sharing and failover capabilities.
- Leverage design that uses alternative systems when it detects a spike in traffic or increase in user load for an existing system.
- Architect store and forward techniques to allow the request to be stored when the target is offline, and send it when its back online.
- Stateless transactions and requests makes the application more scalable. Design applications using stateless session beans improve the scalability.
- Business logic needs be loosely coupled with web tier, hence deploying the application components on the separate node is easier. SOA provides scalability at the integration layer by loose coupling.
- Distribute business components by deploying multiple machines, which can be accessed by the web tier components. This will increase the application's scalability as well.
- Adopt REST-based integrations rather than heavyweight alternatives, such as **Simple Object Access Protocol (SOAP)** or **Application Programming Interface (API)** calls. Using lightweight alternatives, such as REST-based services, are fast, they transfer less data, and are more scalable.
- Minimize the number of static assets, such as images, JavaScript, **Cascading Style Sheets (CSS)**, required by the application. This can be achieved by compressing and merging them to form a minimal set.
- Leverage AJAX-based asynchronous models for server invocations for partial page refresh.
- Leverage on-demand pagination features, where the data required for the second page is fetched only when the user requests the page.

- Leverage lightweight alternatives, such as JSON over XML for service invocations, and do the service invocations only when needed.
- Reduce the amount of data transferred over the wire. Switching to lightweight alternatives, such as the JSON format for web data exchange.
- Design services to be modular and reusable so that they can be easily scaled.
- Scale out UIs by adding multiple nodes to web servers, asset, and media servers. The inbuilt caching of web servers should be leveraged for better performance and scalability.
- Establish smart caching to cache the frequently used data/query results in the application tier to avoid costly APIs.
- Avoid chatty APIs and batch the requests to minimize server round-trips. The fewer the calls, the less the load on the server and hence it will be more scalable.

Checklist

The checklist for the capture of requirements is as follows:

- Are scalability targets identified and approved by key stakeholders?
- Are the targets for throughput and response time identified?
- Do the objectives differentiate between actual scalability and observed scalability?
- Are the scalability targets assessed for rationality?
- Are the expectations of the stakeholders established for what is feasible in the architecture?
- Are all scalability targets defined within the context of the organizational workload?
- Is a framework established to identify the expected scalability and how they combine to produce overall scalability dashboards?
- Is a solution to collect management and instrumentation information devised on actual scalability and compared to organizations scalability requirements?
- Is the data collated adequate to identify potential root causes for scalability bottlenecks?

The checklist for architecture definition is:

- Has enough testing and analysis been completed to understand the likely scalability capabilities of the application?
- Is the major potential scalability problem in your architecture established?

- What workload can your application handle? Are the different classes of workload prioritized?
- How far can the proposed architecture be scaled without major architecture updates?
- Are the scalability-related assumptions identified?
- Has the architecture been reviewed for common scalability bottlenecks?

Scalability KPIs/KRAs

- Ability to scale to support up to X, for example, 50,000,000 unique browsers in any given calendar month by 2020
- Ability to scale up to X, for example, 2 million active registrations
- Ability to support a frequency of up to X, for example, 20 sessions for each unique browser in any given calendar month
- Support up to X, for example, 50 page impressions served per browser session
- Support up to X, for example, 250 million page impressions in any given calendar month
- Support up to X, for example, 5,000 concurrent users at peak periods
- Support an average of X , for example, 20 minutes per user session
- Support up to X, for example, 250,000 bulk add file uploads per calendar month
- Support up to X, for example, 50 concurrent bulk add and image file uploads in peak periods
- Support an average of X, for example, 20 images per upload

KPIs

The following KPI's are as follows:

- Throughput: How many transactions per hour does the system need to be able to handle?
- Year-on-year growth requirements
- Storage: Amount of data the system is required to archive

Availability

Availability is defined as the timespan that the application functions normally. It is scored as the percentage of total application downtime over a specified period.

Availability is affected by faults and exceptions, hardware issues, malicious attacks, maintenance, and upgrades.

Availability is the timespan that the system is operational and available for its end users. Availability is established as few appllctions are architected with expected downtime for activities like database upgrades and backups.

Key drivers

The following lists key drivers as:

- A physical tier such as database or application may fail or become unresponsive, causing the entire system to go offline.
- Denial of Service: **Denial of Service (DoS)** attacks prevent authorized users from accessing the application. It interrupts operations due to massive loads, often due to large processing, or network congestion.
- Inappropriate use of resources can decrease availability. For example, resources acquired early and held for a long time causes resource starvation and an inability to handle additional requests.
- Frequent updates, such as security rollouts or application upgrades, can reduce the availability of the application.
- Faults or issues in the application can cause a system-wide failure.
- Hardware or network faults can cause the application to be unavailable.
- Minimize loss due to downtime and outages.
- Natural disaster or unforeseen circumstances can disrupt business continuity.
- End user satisfaction and loyalty is affected by the availability of business-critical functions, process, and services.
- Competitive advantage is lost if there is no maximum availability of software and services.
- Adhere to laws and regulations in domains, such as healthcare for mission-critical applications.
- Adhere to **service level agreements (SLAs)** promised to clients.
- The impact on an organization's brand value.

Methodology

This process involves the following key aspects:

Availability requirements: Consolidate the complete list of availability requirements from business and IT stakeholders and establish the availability model. Collect various sources, load volume, and geographies for which availability SLAs are applicable. Special-case scenarios, such as geo-specific variations or web page/transaction-specific variations, also need to be collated by interacting with stakeholders.

The availability SLA can be derived from responses to questions such as:

- What is the maximum time period before which the business is severely impacted?
- What are industry and domain benchmarks for availability?
- What is the business/financial cost for a one minute outage?
- What is the acceptable data loss? This helps us in understanding RPO.
- Are scheduled outages acceptable?
- How much of an outage is tolerable?
- What are end users' availability expectations, based on surveys?
- Are there any analyst recommendations for application availability?

The following is the availability establishment process illustrated:

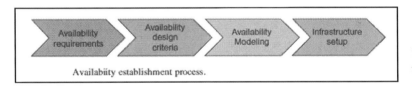

Availability establishment process.

Establish availability design criteria: Availability design criteria should cover various aspects of availability, such as hardware design, software design, operations process, and so on.

The following are the key design aspects listed:

- Design for failure
- Design for handling downtime and recovery
- Design for business continuity and continuous operations

Availability models: Develop availability models to simulate the real-world use cases. The model should factor in all possible failures and should simulate system performance and throughput in these scenarios. The simulation models should help the governance team establish availability policies.

Infrastructure setup: Availability policies obtained from simulation models are leveraged to create a robust and reliable infrastructure. Similarly, leverage the design criteria in software component design. Essentially, the infrastructure and software design should be architected to satisfy the business needs and SLAs.

Solution options

The solution options are as follows:

- The application is designed with a hot standby configuration for high availability. In the case of the primary servers going down, the load balancer will be able to route the request to secondary/hot standby nodes. Make the system more available so if one node is down, another node can take over the work.
- The load balancer is configured to route traffic to hot standby in case the primary reaches its threshold. The load balancer policies should be optimized to distribute the burden and failover to standby instances in the event of issues with the primary node.
- The transaction manager component increases availability and reliability by ensuring the application is always in a consistent state and through a strategy for handling certain classes of failures.
- The design should be stateless, so when a stateless server fails, its work can be routed to a different server without implications for state management.
- The ability to prevent application failures in the event of service(s) failures is commonly architected via redundancy. This can be achieved through fault tolerance techniques, such as active and passive replication.
- A robust monitoring infrastructure set up to frequently do a health check of all internal systems, such as the web server, application server, and database servers. Develop an internal and external monitoring and alerting infrastructure. This serves as an early warning indicator and helps the operations team to respond quickly in case of issues. Continuous real-time monitoring of internal and external systems is essential to identify and fix production issues.
- Ensure a **disaster recovery (DR)** site is present, and that it has a mirror replica of the code and data from the main site. The load balancer is configured to route the requests to the DR site during peak traffic. A geographically separate and redundant site to fail over in the case of natural disasters such as hurricane or floods.
- Recommended HA configurations for the database can be set up and configured. This includes clusters, data replication, and all other configuration proposed by the product vendor.

- Avoid chatty conversations with upstream services to minimize data transfer.
- An open-source caching framework, Memcached, can be leveraged to cache the database records and search results. Additionally, a distributed and cluster cache can be implemented for handling large data.
- Design a failover support for the tiers in the architecture. For example, leverage network load balancing for web servers to distribute the load and prevent requests being directed to a server which may be down.
- Leverage RAID components to mitigate failure in the event of a disk failure.
- Reduce the attack surface area, to minimize interruption from DoS attacks. Leverage instrumentation to establish unintended behavior, and deploy comprehensive validation. Leverage circuit breakers to increase resilience.
- Design for exception handling in order to recover from failures.
- Define the trust boundaries and ensure that sub-systems deploy access controls or firewalls, as well as data validation, to increase availability and resiliency.
- Handle unreliable network connections by designing components with occasionally-connected capabilities.

Checklist

The checklist for the capture of requirements is as follows:

- Ability to have mission critical systems with a percentage uptime of X, for example, 99.2% per month. Critical systems are defined as:
  - Ad placement (storefront, paper production, auto-publish, bulk upload)
  - Core search
  - Transactions
  - Ad management (renew)
  - Notifications
  - Lead generation
- Ability to have non-mission critical systems with a percentage uptime of X, for example, 98.3% per month.
- Ability to schedule downtime for maintenance on the site and/or components/systems
- Have the key stakeholders signed-off the availability requirements?
- Are the requirements driven by business goals and needs?
- Can requirements be met by the selected software and hardware platform?

- Are the strategies for business continuity and disaster recovery defined?
- Do stakeholders have realistic expectations pertaining to unplanned downtime?
- Do requirements consider different classes of service?
- Do requirements strike a balance between business goals and cost?
- Do requirements take into account future business needs such as moving to a longer day?
- What is the business/financial cost for a one minute outage?
- How much of an outage is acceptable?
- Are scheduled outages tolerable?
- Do availability requirements consider batch availability and online?
- Do requirements take into account variations, such as period end?
- What are industry and domain benchmarks for availability?
- What are end users' availability expectations based on surveys?
- What is the maximum timeframe before which the business is severely impacted? This helps in understanding RTO.
- What is the acceptable data loss? This helps in understanding RPO.
- Are there analyst recommendations for application availability?
- What is the business/financial cost for a one minute outage?
- What is the maximum time period before which the business is severely impacted? This helps in understanding RTO.
- Are there any analyst recommendations for application availability?
- What is the acceptable data loss? This helps us in understanding RPO.
- How much of an outage is tolerable?
- What are end users availability expectations based on surveys?
- Are scheduled outages acceptable?

The checklist for architecture definition are as follows:

- Is emphasis given to restoring data from incomplete or corrupt backups?
- Does the application respond elegantly to faults, including logging and reporting them appropriately?
- Does the solution establish the time needed to recover from failure?
- Does the backup technique provide transactional integrity of restored data?
- Does the target architecture meet the availability requirements?
- Does the backup support online backup, with acceptable degradation in performance?

- Is a standby site defined, if appropriate? Is the standby site identical to the primary site or with reduced performance?
- Have you established the mechanisms to switch from production to the standby site?
- Is the impact of the availability solution on performance assessed and acceptable?
- Is the architecture evaluated for bottlenecks, single points of failure, and other weaknesses?
- Does the fault tolerant model extend to all vulnerable entities in the landscape?

KPIs

The following KPI's are:

- Availability: Application availability including the weekends, holidays, maintenance times, and failures
- Geographic location: Connection requirements and the restrictions of a local network prevail
- Offline requirement: Time available for offline operations including batch processing and system maintenance
- Length of time between failures
- Recoverability: This is the time needed to be able to resume operation in the event of fault or exceptions
- Resilience: The reliability characteristics of the system and sub-components

Capacity

Capacity defines the ways in which the systems may be expected to scale-up by increasing hardware capacity based on the organisation's volume projections. For example, transactions per seconds, customers online, response time, and so on.

Capacity is delivering sufficient functionality required by the the end users. A request for a web service to supply 2,000 requests per second, when that server is only capable of 200 requests per second, will not succeed. This is because the server is unable to handle the requested capacity.

Architecture cannot provide sufficient capacity with a single node, and operations personnel need to deploy multiple nodes with a similar configuration to meet business capacity needs.

Key drivers

The following lists:

- **NFR on forecasted demand are incorrect**: Due to the fact that demand volumes change with time and after the NFRs were initially established; or perhaps the process of converting the request to technical transactions was incorrect; or demand was reduced due to budget restrictions.
- **NFR definitions are not comprehensive:** Limited definition for the response times attribute have been met. Other attributes also define the performance of a service and hence its quality. These include the stability and consistency of the service. These all need to be modeled when defining the NFRs.
- **NFRs can't be measured:** The NFRs are modeled in the design stage. Lack of tracking and monitoring will lead to NFRs being unenforceable.
- **There are no limitations on the infrastructure:** This is equivalent to handing infinite infrastructure to either your internal delivery team or operations team.

Methodology

The methodology listed is as follows:

Properly estimated and appropriately sized infrastructure components are an essential requirement for achieving scalability, availability, and optimal performance.

The main steps in capacity planning are as follows:

- **Demand analysis:** In this step, we will collate all data about the current demand, workload, trends, and all aspects of usages of infrastructure such as CPU, memory, and the network. The key process steps are collecting infrastructure usage statistics using tools, preparing a questionnaire for each of the infrastructure elements, and compiling observations from all key stakeholders.
- **Current capacity analysis**: Once we get all aspects of present and future demands of the user load on systems, we can analyze and determine whether the existing capability of the systems can meet those demands. We can establish the threshold and benchmark values for establishing whether the utilization of critical resources are optimum. We will relook at the current resource utilization for an extended duration and determine the following values:
  - Resources that are underutilized
  - Resources that are heavily utilized

A comparison of utilization against the threshold and benchmark values and an end-to-end analysis to identify the bottleneck. The inputs from the above values can be used to optimize capacity planning. For example, any resources that are underutilized for an extended duration of time can be consolidated or virtualized to increase utilization.

Similarly, resources that are consistently over-utilized can be planned for a capacity upgrade. The capacity can be increased for bottleneck resources in the landscape.

- **Future capacity planning:** Leveraging historical data, trend analysis, and future workload prediction models can be used to arrive at the required server capacity. In addition to a prediction model, we should consider the vendor recommendations for capacity. Most of the vendors for hardware and software provide recommended configurations for optimal use of their products. This information will be used as key input in coming up with final capacity numbers. Hence, a combination of predicted capacity and vendor recommendations will be used to arrive at final capacity numbers.

Please note that it is important to test the target capacity values with the simulation models and expected workload. There may be many factors that cannot be accurately determined during the capacity planning exercise, mainly because the application is still under development, including:

- Number, complexity, and data transfer rate with interfacing systems
- Use of design patterns and number of tiers/layers in the architecture
- Overhead caused by replication and cache/session replication
- Any changes to workloads assumed during capacity planning
- Overhead caused by batch jobs, offline reports, search crawlers, and application/system monitoring tools on the enterprise application
- Use of open-source or COTS tools and frameworks in the engagement

All these factors will influence the overall performance, and so the initially estimated capacity/sizing numbers may need to be revisited. It is recommended to treat capacity planning as a two-step process: firstly, perform an initial assessment based on the future resource use and stakeholder interviews; secondly, test the new capacity leveraging simulations during the QA phases. This is to ensure that the planned capacity adequately meets future demands. During this stage, the capacity numbers may need to be fine-tuned based on application performance.

Solution options

The solution options are stated as follows:

- The architecture is designed to support both vertical as well as horizontal scalability.
- To handle more client requests, the application is scaled by deploying additional web containers on multiple machines.
- The application server will be clustered, which provides the ability to add processing capability by simply adding instances to the cluster.
- Using connection pooling for database and resource pooling improves the scalability of applications.
- Architect applications using stateless session beans to improve the scalability of the application.
- Additional application or database servers can be added (horizontal scaling) to improve the scalability of the application.
- The business logic should be loosely coupled with a web tier, so deploying the components on separate nodes is simplified.
- We can distribute the business components by deploying on multiple machines, and they can be accessed by the web tier components remotely. This will increase the application's scalability as well.

Checklist

The checklist for the capture of requirements is as follows:

- What types of technology patterns are available for the transactions? Are the volumes higher during a predefined time during the day (for example, the afternoon), week, month or year?
- What are the different types of transactions that can execute? For the transaction, what are the hourly, daily, weekly, monthly, yearly volumes?
- What is the current traffic between servers in the legacy application?
- What are the current challenges in the legacy application?
- Are there any peak traffic trends expected for the new online platform?
- What transaction volume growth is expected?
- Will additional applications leverage the services? What happens if the point-of-sale components start trying to use these services? Can additional volume be handled?

- What is the average response time of the current database? What is the growth projection?
- What is the size of product data expected to be stored in the product database? What is the growth projection?
- What is the size of maximum concurrent users? What is the growth projection?
- What would be the maximum number of expected registered users and public users for the new site? What is the growth projection?
- What is the approximate number of page views for each session? What is the growth projection?
- What is the approximate total number of web pages for a new application? What is the growth projection?
- What is the approximate number of web components and business components, and their complexity levels? What is the growth projection?
- What is the average response time?
- What are the peak transactions per hour?
- What is the maximum number of database users? What is the growth projection?
- Are there any future plans for database migration or consolidation?
- What is the number of maximum concurrent users?
- What is the current traffic between the web server, application server, and database server?
- Which application is using the bulk of the bandwidth?
- What is the traffic between the application server and upstream and downstream systems?
- Are there any seasonal or behavior trends related to peak traffic?
- What are the applications and servers that are expected to be onboard, and what are their data demands?
- High service time, if the service time is more than 40 seconds on average
- High network packet drop rate, if the drop rate is more than three package

KPIs

The KPI's are as follows:

- Throughput: Number of peak transactions the application needs to handle
- Storage: Volume of data the system will page/persist at runtime to disk. This relates to the memory/disk

- Year-on-year growth requirements (users, processing & storage)
- e-channel growth projections
- Different types of things, for example, activities or transactions supported, volumes on an hourly, daily, weekly, monthly, yearly basis
- Are volumes higher during predefined parts of the day (for example, at lunch), week, month or year?
- Transaction volume growth expected and additional volumes you will be able to handle

Security

Security is the ability to avoid malicious events and incidents to the designed system usage, and prevent loss of information. Establishing proper security enhances the reliability of a system by reducing the likelihood of an attack succeeding and disrupting critical functions. Security protects assets and prevent unauthorized access to sensitive data. The factors affecting security are integrity and confidentiality. The features used to secure applications are authorization, authentication, logging, auditing and encryption.

Key drivers

The key drivers are as follows:

- Swindling of user identity
- Information disclosure and loss of sensitive data.
- Damage due to malicious attacks such as cross-site scripting or SQL injection
- Repudiation of user actions
- Interruption of business critical operations due to DoS attacks

Methodology

The methodology and process for establishing a comprehensive security for enterprise applications are listed in the following diagram:

- **Security analysis**: The first step in security is to understand all the security requirements in the analysis phase. Organizational security policies and standards will be incorporated into the program as security requirements.

- Different potential risks that will be faced by the enterprise will be considered. The security team will come up with policies and designs for all identified security requirements. Security policies will outline the security measures that need to be covered in software and at hardware levels, such as ports, protocols, firewalls, and encryption standards. In this step, we will establish a comprehensive security checklist that will be used for implementation and verification by the development and testing teams.

- **Threat modeling**: All internal and external threats will be analyzed during this stage. The main risks and threats for the enterprise applications are identified and modeled. This information will be used to provide recommendations to devise controls and policies. The threats will be categorized and prioritized based on the probability of occurrence and the impact of the threat. Some critical external threats include Distributed Denial of Service (DDoS), worms and Trojan Horses, phishing attacks, natural disasters. Some of the internal threats include identity theft and physical threats. An increasing trend is phishing attacks on e-mail, client-side request manipulation, and spam generated from social media websites.

- **Security design:** Different scenarios for the major tenets, such as confidentiality, integrity, and availability, will be identified. Detailed security principles and security control policies will be outlined based on recommendations and assessments done in previous stages. For example, a man-in-the-middle attack scenario can compromise the information integrity, and DDoS will impact the availability. For each of the user scenarios, a security policy will be designed and mapped. Security policies will be aimed mainly at prevention, detection, and the recovery from security events and incidents. Security policies should provide comprehensive coverage for all kinds of threat scenarios.

- **Security implementation and QA**: The security checklist identified in the analysis stage should be strictly followed during application development. Based on security guidelines and policies, comprehensive security measures will be implemented at all tiers and for all software and hardware components. Configuration changes should be done at the server end to enforce the prescribed policies. Different static code analysis tools scan the code for potential security issues and should be leveraged. Similarly, black-box penetration testing tools and scripts should also be used for uncovering application vulnerabilities. Internal and external ethical hackers and security experts should be engaged in carrying out sophisticated security tests and vulnerability assessment.

- **Security monitoring**: Security is a continuous and ongoing process, and therefore, even after the application is deployed, the application should be closely monitored for all kinds of security incidents and events. Security policies and patches must be updated on a timely basis for maximum protection.

The security establishment process is shown in the following diagram:

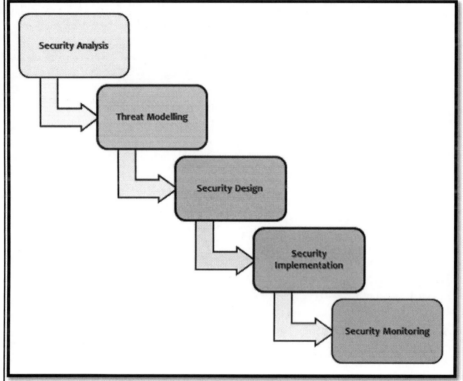

Solution options

The solution options are as follows:

- Leverage authorization and authentication to prevent spoofing of identity and identify trust boundaries
- Design various controls to prevent access to sensitive data or system
- Establish monitoring and instrumentation to analyze user interaction for critical operations
- Protect against damage by ensuring that you validate all inputs for type, range, and length, and sanitize principles
- Partition users into anonymous, identified, and authenticated, and leverage monitoring and instrumentation for audit instrumentation, logging and root cause analysis

- Leverage encryption, sign-sensitive data, and use secure transport channels
- Reduce session timeouts and implement solutions to detect and mitigate attacks
- The security will be provided through DMZ using an inner and outer firewall; application and database servers will be behind the inner firewall, and the web server will be behind an outer firewall in the DMZ
- The architecture uses form-based authentication for the web tier, and the security logic is implemented in a reusable business component in the application tier.
- SSL will provide the desired security for sending sensitive information to critical systems, like merchant bank and market place
- Leverage esmsage-level encryption, digital signatures and transport-layer security - SSL
- The application will use LDAP for authentication on the web tier and will use role-based security on the web and business tier for authorization
- Authorization is controlled access to information in the application once a user is identified and authenticated
- Authentication: Identification of an end-user in the system and validation that the user is telling the truth
- Auditing: Instrumentation and monitoring of security
- Integrity: Protection against improper modification of information in transit or storage
- Confidentiality: Protection against inappropriate disclosure of data during transit and storage.
- User or security role should be given the lowest privilege for a resource or function. Privileges will not be elevated automatically by direct or indirect means, and therefore one should maintain a default deny policy
- Enforce appropriate security policies at all tiers, components, systems, and services using appropriate security policies, techniques, and operations; a security policy at each layer is different from one layer to another, making it difficult for the hacker to break the system; identify and fix the most vulnerable point in the end-to-end chain of components.
- The security framework should support a standards-based plug-in model wherein it is possible to architect pluggable extensions to improve the security position
- All software and hardware resources and functions should be categorized into various security classifications, and access should be restricted to users with appropriate roles and privileges
- Pluggable extensions would be required to re-use the security framework in different environments and to comply with local regulations and laws

- The system should provide a holistic view of administration features to manage essential security functionality
- The application should allow users only a single authentication point. Back-door entry functionality and shortcut URLs should be avoided
- Data entered by the user must be thoroughly validated and cleansed at different levels; data must also be properly encrypted when stored and transferred to various layers
- Minimize entry points for end users and retain a minimum amount of data, service, and functionality exposed to unauthorized end users
- Design contingency plans for all possible failure scenarios: It is feasible to minimize the impact of security incidents by using robust error handling routines, data backups, a disaster recovery (DR) environment, and in-depth defense

Best practice:

- **SQL Injection**: Prepared or dynamic SQL statements
- **Cross Site Scripting**: JSF validation, avoid JavaScripts, and avoid frame/iframes
- **Denial of Service**: Service Request Queue Technique, limiting the number of concurrent requests, and queuing all excess requests
- **Man-in-the-Middle**: Using SSL, avoid frames/iframes, avoid URL rewriting

Checklist

The checklist for the capture of requirements is as follows:

- Are the requirements for data integrity identified?
- Are the sensitive resources in the application identified?
- Are the sets of principles for accessing the resources identified?
- Is a security policy of an application established, including entities, actions, resources and information integrity needs?
- Has a threat model to identify the security risks been identified?
- Are the stakeholders appraised, through example scenarios, so that they understand the security policy and the security risk?
- Is the security policy kept simple?
- Are security requirements reviewed with security SMEs?

The checklist for architecture definition is:

- Has each identified threat been addressed to the level desired/required?
- Have you leveraged as much third-party security technology as possible?
- Has an integrated end-to-end architecture for security been produced?
- Have all the security principles been thought-out when designing the infrastructure?
- Have you established how the security breaches will be detected and the protocol to recover from breaches?
- Are the results of the security standpoint for all the affected views applied?
- Have SMEs reviewed the security solution?

KPIs

The following KPI's are:

- Authentication: Correct identification of parties attempting to access systems and protection of systems from unauthorized parties
- Authorization: Mechanism required to authorize users to perform different functions within the systems
- Encryption (data in flight and at rest): All external communications between the application data server and clients to be encrypted
- Data confidentiality: All data must be protectively established, secured and archived
- Compliance: The process to confirm system compliance with the organization's security standards and policies

Maintainability

Maintainability is the ability of the application to go through changes with a fair degree of effortlessness. This attribute is the flexibility with which the application can be modified, for fixing issues, or to add new functionality with a degree of ease. These changes could impact components, services, functionality, and interfaces when modifying for fixing issues, or to meet future demands. Maintainability has a direct baring on the the time it takes to restore the application to normal status following a failure or an upgrade. Enlightened maintainability attributes will enhance availability and reduce runtime defects. Maintainability is a function of the overall software quality attributes. This is why a large portion of the organizational IT budget is spent on maintenance of critical software quality attributes. More maintainable applications will have a lower TCO.

Key drivers

The key drivers are as follows:

- The code base of the application is large, unmanageable, complex, brittle, and refactoring is burdensome due to regression
- Lack of documentation hinders usage and future upgrades
- Implementation does not have an automated regression test framework
- Extreme dependencies among tiers, layers, and components, and incorrect coupling of classes prevents replacement and updates, and can cause changes to flow through the entire system
- Leveraging direct communication prevents changes to the physical architecture i.e layers, tiers, and components
- Interdependency on bespoke applications of features such as authentication and authorization prevents reuse and hampers maintenance
- The implementation of components and modules are not cohesive, which makes them difficult to maintain and upgrade, and causes unnecessary dependencies on other entities in the system

Methodology

Maintainability requirements are defined in terms of the compliance with standards, frameworks and best practice. Maintainability requirements should also make conformance with these guidelines clear.

Solution options

The solution options are as follows:

- The logical separation of the application into different tiers (client, presentation, business logic, integration and EIS tier) allows a system to be flexible and easily maintained. When there are any changes in presentation, it will be done at the presentation tier, and it will not affect the other tiers. If there are any business logic changes, only EJB component business logic get changed, and it will not affect other tiers, and vice versa.

- MVC pattern leverages command patterns at the web tier (JSF backing bean classes) for handling web events. Therefore, when new functionalities are added to the system, it will not affect the existing system. We can easily create a new web action by developing a new backing bean class and configure it in a faces-config.xml file. Even modifying the existing functionality becomes easier by changing the respective backing bean classes.
- Object orientation like encapsulation, inheritance, low coupling, and high cohesion are leveraged in application design. Any changes to subsystems will have less impact on systems which are using it as long the interfaces remain the same.
- Independence of interface from implementation permits the substitution of different implementations for the same functionality.
- Design applications consisting of layers or areas of concern that clearly demarcate the UI, business processes, and data access layers.
- Design cross-layer dependencies by using abstractions instead of concrete classes, and minimize dependencies between tiers, layers, and components.
- Define and establish a proper communication protocol, model, and format.
- Design pluggable architecture that facilitate easy maintenance, and improves testing processes
- Architect interfaces to provide plug-in architecture to maximize flexibility and extensibility.
- Leverage built-in container and platform functions and features wherever possible instead of custom application.
- Architecture to have high cohesion and low coupling in order to maximize flexibility and facilitate reusability.
- Establish methodology to manage dynamic business processes and dynamic business rules, by using workflow engine for dynamic business processes.
- Solution business components to implement the rules if only the business rule values tend to change; or implement an external source, such as a business rules engine, if the business decision rules tend to change.
- Invest in automation suites for QA as the system are created and deployed. This will pay off as a QA of the system's functionality, and as documentation on what the various parts of the system do and how they work in collaboration.
- Provide artifacts to explains the structure of the application. Proper documentation includes architecture diagrams, interfaces, class diagrams, sequence diagrams, and coding guidelines, are the key criterion for maintainable IT systems.

Checklist

The checklist for the capture of requirements is as follows:

- Do all entities have an identifier, responsibilities, and interfaces?
- Do all exchange takes place via well-defined interfaces and adapters?
- Do the entities demonstrate an appropriate level of coupling & cohesion?
- Are the key business scenarios established and leveraged to validate the system's behavior?
- Is the coverage of your architecture checked to ensure it meets the requirements?
- Is consideration given to how the architecture will cope with future change scenarios?
- Are the approaches and methodologies to design defined so that the designers and implementers can follow them?
- Are a set of third-party software elements to be leveraged across the implementations established?
- Is the strategy outlined for migrating from the current environment to the target environment?
- Is the migration strategy outlined for moving the workload into the target system?
- How will you handle data synchronization?
- Is the system backed up procedure identified? Are you confident that the approach outlined will allow reliable application restoration in an adequate timespan?
- Are the administrators convinced that they will be able to monitor and control the applications in production?
- Do the administrators have a clear understanding of the procedures they need to run the application?
- How will performance KPI & metrics for the application elements be captured?

The checklist for architecture definition:

- Are development standards leveraged (for example, schemes, programming, database approach, recognizable nomenclature, user interfaces)?
- Are the actions built into the interface consistent?
- Are the algorithms and processing optimized?

- Are the I/O operations solutions in distinct modules in order to separate the processing of data from the retrieval of data?
- Are the subsystems distributed?
- Are the check processes or watchdogs established?
- Is the operations team capable of providing status information?
- Is the data processing divided into sub-transactions?
- Are the input, output, and processing, implemented separately?
- Are the possible machine dependencies solutions in distinct modules?
- Are the programs well structured and easy to understand?
- Is up-to-date and consistent documentation available?
- Is the critical functionality contained in distinct modules?
- Will data processing be done in parallel?

KPIs

The KPI's are as follows:

- Conformance to design standards, coding standards, best practice, reference architectures, and frameworks.
- Flexibility: The degree to which the system is intended to support change
- Release support: The way in which the system will support the introduction of initial release, phased rollouts and future releases
- Up-to-date and consistent documentation

Manageability

Manageability is the ease with which the administrators can monitor the system, through critical health status exposed through its monitoring capabilities. This is the ability of the system or the group of the system to provide key information to the ops team to be able to debug, analyse and understand the root cause of failures. It deals with compliance with the domain frameworks and policies.

The key is designing an application which is simple to manage, by publishing critical health status information from the monitoring capabilities and for analyzing the root cause of failures.

Key drivers

The following list is as follows:

- Lack of monitoring, instrumentation, and diagnostic information
- Lack of runtime re-configurability
- Lack of troubleshooting tools and diagnostic information
- Lack of tracking ability and health monitoring capability

Methodology

Manageability is the simplicity with which the entities of an applications can be monitored for health status and instrumentation.

This process involves the following key aspects:

- Ability to leverage a monitoring and management applications to get a single view of the entire landscape of your enterprise applications
- Get alerts, events and notifications as the thresholds are approached, for example, storage, CPU, and memory
- Remotely control systems and applications, and be able to spin new virtual machines at the click of a mouse
- Create a rich graphical dashboard of the main system metrics and KPIs

Solution options

The solution options are as follows:

- Design to publish data about errors and state changes in order to enable health status monitoring, management and issue resolutions.
- Establish a health status model that captures the state changes based on application performance, and leverage this health model for health instrumentation requirements.
- Design monitoring, such as performance counters, alerts, and events, that detects state changes and publish this through standard management instrumentation capabilities.
- Create a snapshot of the system's state to leverage for troubleshooting and include instrumentation that can be activated to provide detailed operational and functional reports.

- Design the auditing of application data that will be useful for debugging and issue resolution. A good logging mechanism will be critical for identifying fatal or error conditions.
- Enable tracing in the web tier to troubleshoot errors and exceptions conditions.
- Leverage standard frameworks to provide logging and tracing support in the implementation, though dependency injection and **Aspect Oriented Programming (AOP)**.
- Establish a method for monitoring the system behaviors and heath. Consider leveraging monitoring tools, such as systems center.
- Leverage tools like Tivoli software to provide extensive monitoring and management capability for the entire application landscape.
- Plan for instrumentation and profiling of implementation to ensure that it meets the quality thresholds and standards.

Checklist

The checklist for the capture of requirements is as follows:

- A defined set of operational management information KPIs and metrics that the organisation should be able to track has been identified. These KPIs will cover key people, processes, and technology aspects.
- The management and monitoring capability can generate the health information for the entire enterprise landscape (for example, CPU utilization, memory utilization, free disk space, and the size of an incoming call queue).
- The management and monitoring capability can aggregate and analyse the gathered health status information for the entire application landscape.
- The management and monitoring system can mark threshold limits for major run-time KPIs and metrics, and generate alerts and notification to improving the operational KPIs and metrics of the enterprise.
- There is be a methodology by which aggregated information is leveraged to improve processes and skills.
- Are back-up and recovery procedures defined for the periodic saving of a coherent copies data ?
- Does the backup procedure define when the data sets and database need to be secured, and how long these back-ups should be retained?
- Are specific standards and frameworks defined for input, batch processing, online processing, and output ?

- Are development standards leveraged (for example, schemes, programming, database approach, recognizable nomenclature, user interfaces)?
- Are the actions built into the interface consistent?
- Are the I/O operation solutions in distinct modules in order to separate the processing of data from the retrieval of data?
- Are the check processes or watchdogs established ?
- Is the operations team capable of providing status information?
- Is up-to-date and consistent documentation available?

The checklist for architecture definition:

- Is a methodology to move from the current environment to the target environment defined?
- Is a migration strategy to transfer the user load to the target system defined?
- Is the backup procedure identified?
- Does the defined methodology allow reliable restoration of the systems in an acceptable timespan?
- Will the operations team be able to monitor the application landscape in the runtime environment?
- Do the administrators have a full understanding of the SLAs and processes for the landscape?
- Does the solution take into account the time needed to recover from failures, for example, to restore from backup if necessary?
- Does the backup methodology ensure transactional integrity of restored data?
- Does the backup methodology support online backup, with tolerable degradation in application performance? Is it feasible to take the system offline to perform data backups?
- Is a process established for restoring data from corrupt or incomplete backups?
- Will the system be able to respond gracefully to exceptions, logging, and reporting them into the management and monitoring solution?
- Is a standby site in the DR plan defined? Is the standby site identical to the primary site, or does it offer reduced performance? If the latter, is this reduced performance acceptable to the users?
- Have you established a methodology for switching from the primary to backup site?
- Has the impact assessment of the availability solution on functionality and performance been done and is it acceptable?
- Is the architecture assessed for single points of failure and other bottlenecks?

- Does the fault-tolerant model apply to all vulnerable components of the landscape?

KPIs

The KPI's are:

- System must maintain full traceability of transactions
- Audited objects and audited database fields to be included for auditing
- File characteristics, such as size before, size after, and structure
- User and transactional time stamps, and so on
- Design for events and alerts as thresholds are approached (for example, storage, memory, and processor)
- Remotely manage the landscape and create new virtual instances at the click of a mouse
- Valuable graphical dashboards for all key applications metrics

Reliability

Reliability is the characteristics of an application to continue functioning in an expected manner over time. Reliability is scored as the probability that the application will not fail and that it will keep functioning for a defined timespan. It is the ability of the application to maintain its performance over a specific timespan. Unreliable software fails frequently, and specific tasks are more prone to failure because they cannot be restarted or resumed.

Key drivers

The key drivers are as follows:

- The application fails due to inaccessibility of externalities, such as applications, databases or networks
- The system crashes or becomes unresponsive
- The output is inconsistent
- Improper and inadequate testing of applications and systems
- Lack of a change management processes
- Lack of the directorate and monitoring and analysis capability
- Operational issues, exceptions and errors

- Lack of standards, best practice, and frameworks during the implementation phase
- Lack of quality software engineering frameworks and processes
- Integration with external third party services or systems
- Variations in operating conditions, for example, usage level changes and peak overloads
- Hardware failures, for example, servers, memory, disks, CPUs, controllers, and network devices
- Operational and environmental problems, for example, power, natural disasters, flood, cooling, fire, security failures

Methodology

Reliability is the ability to operate without faults and failures and to be able to recover from faults and exceptions. This includes precise data and transformations, flawless state management, and non-corrupting recovery from failure events. Creating reliable systems depends on the entire SDLC from the architecture to early design, through the build, to deployment and ongoing maintenance.

This process involves the following key aspects:

- **Build Management and instrument information into the system**:

    In the architecture stage, it is critical to include health monitoring information for the application. This information includes resource consumption, response times, status conditions, and warnings. Monitoring is a critical best practice that enables continues analysis, identification, and isolation of system failure problems before they can occur and crippling the infrastructure

- **Leverage redundancy for reliability**:

    Design methodology for achieving reliability are based on redundancy of software and hardware components. The redundancy ensures non-corrupting recovery from various failure events.

They might be double or triple redundant components running in parallel with common validation checks. The alternative technique is leveraging clustering, load balancing, replication, and protecting complex functions with transactions to ensure integrity.

Redundant hardware components: Best practice redunduncy strategy includes arrays of disks, network interfaces, and power supplies. With such an infrastructure, module failures can occur without affecting the overall reliability.

- **Leverage quality development tools**:

  Software tools and frameworks should help with development of fault-tolerant and robust applications and provide a UI rich IDE for coding, QA and deploying distributed applications.

- **Leverage robust error handling and health checks**:

  An error handling capability is a critical source of failure resolution in many distributed architectures. A well-architected application must respond to exception conditions in a systemetic way. The application also needs to run scheduled health checks on a continuous basis.The process consists of identification of error condition, determination of the resolution, and gracefully continue running the application.

- **Remove single point of failures in the design**:

  A reliable system provides a significant benefit: such an application is much simpler to enhance, while an unreliable application costs much more to change.

- **Leverage SDLC process**:

  Leverage consistent, repeatable, software development methodology which will lead to a reliable application. A formal process establishes a detailed analysis leading to innovation and discovery. An efficient data center leverages documented processes for software development, capacity planning, configuration management, change management, incident management, network and security operations.

Solution options

The solution options are as follows:

- Establish alternatives to detect exceptions and automatically initiate a system failover, or redirect the request to a standby system. Implement code that leverages alternate nodes when a failed request is detected from an existing application.
- Design for instrumentation, such as events or performance counters, that detects performance problems or external system failures and exposes information through standard interfaces, such as, WMI, trace files, and event logs. Log performance, errors, exceptions and auditing information about calls made to other systems and services.
- Establish alternatives to manage unreliable application, failed APIs, and failed transactions. Identify queuing pending requests if the application goes offline.
- Design a store and forward or cached mechanism that allows requests to be stored when the target application is unavailable, and forward when the target is online.
- Design the solution leveraging queuing to provide a reliable alternative for asynchronous APIs.
- The solution should be capable of recovering from an error or exception based on your error and exception strategy
- The primary server serves all the requests, but a backup server is added to route traffic if the primary server goes down or is taken offline for upgrades.
- Data integrity is established with security controls/mechanisms which will prevent the third party from making any unauthorized access and/or changes to data.
- Database transactions ensure data integrity as it will be a full commit or a rollback based on success/failure status.
- The application should be able to go back to a previous version of a system in the event of failure. This depends on good source code management, good version control, and good rollout strategies.
- The application should be able to restore data in the case of loss or corruption. This is vital for many enterprises to go back to just before the incident occurred to avoid the painstaking task of recapturing the data between the last consistent backup and the time the incident occured.
- In the event of an application failure, you may fail-over to an alternative or standby site until the primary is back online. Establish the recoverability of an enterprise by defining the backup entities and contingency roadmap.

Checklist

The checklist for the capture of requirements is as follows:

- An organisational disaster management plan must be created that identifies key people, business functions, systems, and processes and put in place mitigations to cope with disaster.
- The system has sufficient control to revert to earlier version in the event of failed upgrades.
- The data an be backed-up at a frequency proportional to the rate of change of data and stored securely and in controlled conditions both offsite (disaster support) and onsite (quick restore).
- The recovery media, which includes data, source code, and duplicate hard copy materials, is stored in a geographically different location that provides sufficient insulation from regional emergencies whilst still being workable in the event of a natural disaster or incident.
- The recovery media is stored safely, securely and in controlled conditions.
- The business critical applications have a standby site maintained in an operationally ready state. This site is capable of replacing the primary site and can provide a hot fail-over capability.
- Key roles are shared between different people to facilitate recoverability in the case of staff turnover, injury, or illness.
- A methodology exists to QA the disaster management and recoverability on a periodic basis.

The checklist for architecture definition is as follows:

- Are development standards leveraged (for example, schemes, programming, database approach, recognizable nomenclature, and user interfaces)?
- Are the subsystems distributed?
- Are the check processes or watchdogs established?
- Is the operations team capable of providing status information?
- Are the input, output, and processing, implemented separately?
- Are the programs well-structured and easy to understand?
- Is the critical functionality contained in distinct modules?
- Will data processing be done in parallel?
- Has a methodology been defined to move from the current environment to the target environment?

- Has a migration strategy been defined to transfer the workload to the target system?
- Has the application backup procedure been identified?
- Does the defined methodology allow reliable restoration of the systems in an acceptable timespan?
- Will the operations team be able to monitor and control the application landscape in a production environment?
- Do the administrators have full knowledge of the processes to perform for the landscape?
- Does the solution emphasize the time to recover from system failures, for example, restoring backups?
- Does the backup technique ensure transactional integrity of restored data?
- Does the backup technique provide online backups, with acceptable performance degradation?
- Has consideration been given to restoring data from corrupt or incomplete backups?
- Will the application be able to respond elegantly to exceptions, and reporting them into the management and monitoring solution?
- Is a standby site in the DR plan defined? Is the standby site identical to the primary site, or offer reduced performance?
- Are the techniques for switching between primary to standby site defined?
- Has the impact of the availability solution on functionality and performance been assessed?
- Has the architecture been assessed for single points of failure and other bottlenecks?
- Does the fault-tolerant model extend to all entitites in the landscape?

KPIs

The KPI's are as follows:

- The capability of an application to perform the required functions under stated conditions for a specific time period
- Mean time between failures: The acceptable threshold for downtime
- Mean time to recovery: The time available to get the application back online
- Data integrity is the referential integrity in databases
- Application integrity and information integrity during transactions

- Fault trapping (I/O) handling failures and recovery

Extensibility

Extensibility is a characteristic where the architecture, design, and implementation actively caters to future business needs.

Extensible applications have excellent endurance, which avoids the expensive process of procuring large inflexible applications and retiering them due to changes in business needs. Extensibility enables organizations to take advantage of opportunities and respond to risks. While there is a significant difference, extensibility is often confused with modifiability quality. Modifiability means that is possible to change the software, whereas extensibility means that a change has been planned and will be effortless. Adaptability is at times erroneously leveraged with extensibility. However, adaptability deals with how the user interactions with the system are managed and governed.

Key drivers

The key drivers are as follows:

- Interchanging different areas of concern in your design
- Inconsistent or poorly managed development processes
- Lack of corporation between various LOBs involved in the application lifecycle
- Lack of architecture and coding standards
- Legacy application demands can stop refactoring and advances toward a new framework
- Leveraging many systems to implement similar functions instead of sharing functionality, across multiple entities, or across sub-systems

Methodology

Extensibility facilitates application, people, technology, and processes all working together to achieve and objective.

This process involves the following key aspects:

- Manage new responsibilities
- Manage new data and information types
- Manage new or enhanced business entities

Extensibility requirements are outlined in terms of the compliance with standards, best practice, and frameworks. Extensibility requirements should also make clear conformance with these guidelines.

Solution options

The solution options are as follows:

- The logical separation of the application into various tiers (for example, client, presentation, business logic, integration and EIS tiers) allows a system to be flexible and easily maintained. When there are any changes in presentation, it will be done at the presentation tier, and it will not affect the other tiers. If there are any business logic changes, only EJB components business logic get changed, and it will not affect other tiers, and vice versa.
- The MVC architecture leverages command patterns at the web tier (JSF backing bean classes) for handling web events. Therefore, when new functionalities are added to the system, it will not affect the existing system. We can easily create a new web action by developing a new backing bean class and configuring it in a faces-config.xml file. Modifying the existing functionality becomes easy by changing the respective backing bean classes.
- Object orientation like encapsulation, inheritance, high cohesion and low coupling are leveraged in application design. So, the subsystems changes will have less impact on applications which are using it as long the interfaces remain same.
- Independence of interface from implementation permits the substituting of different implementations for the same functionality.
- Design systems and layers that demarcate the system's UI, processes, and data access funtionality.
- Design cross-layer interdependencies by leveraging abstractions rather than concrete implementations, and minimize dependencies between layers and components.
- Design a plug and play architecture that facilitates easy maintenance and upgrades, and improves QA processes. Use APIs enabling plug and play modules or components to maximize flexibility and extensibility.
- Leverage the built-in platform features wherever available instead of custom implementation.
- Design modules to have high cohesion and low coupling to enhance flexibility and provide reusability and replacement.

- Establish the method to manage dynamic processes and dynamic rules, by leveraging workflow engine if the business processes tends to change.
- Solution business components to implement the rules if the rule values are dynamic or an component such as rules engine if the business decision rules are dynamic.
- Provide artifacts that explain the overall structure of the application. Good documentation of the application, which consists of architecture diagrams, interfaces, class diagrams, sequence diagrams, and coding guidelines are the key criterion for maintainable IT systems.
- Identify areas of concern and consolidate them into logical depiction, business, data, and service layers as appropriate.
- Establish a development model with tools and frameworks to provide workflow, and collaboration.
- Establish guidelines for architecture, design and coding standards, and incorporate reviews into your SDLC process to ensure guidelines are diligently implemented.
- Establish a migration roadmap from legacy applications, and isolate applications from interdependencies.
- Expose functionality from layers, subsystems and modules through APIs that other systems and layers can invoke.
- Logical separation of the application into different tiers (client, presentation, business logic, integration and EIS tiers) allows a system to be flexible and easily extensible.
- Leverage design patterns throughout the application architecture.
- OOD, like encapsulation, inheritance, low coupling, and high cohesion are leveraged in application design. This ensures that changes to dependent systems will have less impact on SuD.
- Excellent documentation of the applications (for instance, architecture diagrams, interface agreements, class diagrams, sequence diagrams, coding guidelines, and so on).
- Separation of concerns required, providing a catalogue of services from a registry and allowing various processes to leverage these services through a defined protocol.
- Independency of interface and implementation allows substitution of implementations for the same interface.
- A strategy to separate data and functions addressing various concerns. As the concerns are different, one can update each concern independently.
- Emphasis on runtime design and no hard coding in the application implementation.

Checklist

The checklist for capture of requirements is as follows:

- The application offers a mechanism to facilitate extension of core capabilities by the vendor or end organisation
- The system responsible for persistence is governed by an entity model. The entity models are extensible to allow the modification of entity types or the creation of new entity types to match business needs.
- The application accountable for data processing is governed by a engine or model. The engine is extensible to facilitate refinement of existing processing rules or creation of new rules to match business needs.
- The information processed, derived, stored, and leverage is documented in an model and also includes the relationships between information types.
- There is a set of processes to control the extension of entities, rules, and information types to ensure business continuity
- There is a current state business process model describing how people, technology, and processes collaboratively work together to meet organization needs. This process model will be leveraged in planning, POC, and rollout of future changes to processes.
- Do all entity interactions take place via well-defined connectors and interfaces?
- Do the entities exhibit an appropriate cohesion level?
- Do the entities exhibit an adequate level of coupling?
- Are relevant business scenarios identified and leveraged to validate the applications behaviour?
- Is the functional coverage of the architecture assessed to ensure it meets its busness requirements?
- Has consideration been given as to how the architecture will cope with change scenarios in the future?

The checklist for architecture definition:

- Will the operations team be able to monitor and control the application landscape in a production environment?
- Does the backup technique ensure integrity of restored data?
- Does the backup technique support taking online backups, with acceptable degradation in performance?
- Will the system be able to respond gracefully to errors and exceptions, logging and reporting them into the management and monitoring solution?

- Is a standby site in the DR plan defined? Is the standby site identical to the primary site, or does it offer reduced performance?
- Has the impact of an availability solution on functionality and performance been assessed?
- Has the architecture been assessed for single points of failure and other bottlenecks?
- Do the fault-tolerant guidelines extend to all vulnerable entities in the landscape?
- Are standards, frameworks, and best practice for development established (for example, scheme techniques, programming, database approach, user interfaces)?
- Are the programs parameterized?
- Are logical values leveraged instead of hard coded values?
- Is it possible to modify input, control, processing, and output functions in order to change a way of work?
- Is it possible to configure menu structures?
- Is it feasible to set up the contents of the input screens?
- Is it feasible to set the layout of the input screens?

KPIs

The following KPI's are as follows:

- Handle new information types
- Manage new or changed business entities
- Consume or provide new feeds

Recovery

In the event of a potential disaster, for example, flood, tornado, and so on, the entire facility where the application is hosted may become inoperable. Business-critical applications should have a plan in place to recover from such disasters within a reasonable amount of time. The solution implementing the various processes must be integrated with the existing enterprise disaster recovery plans. The processes must be analysed to understand the criticality of each process to the business, and the impact of loss to the business in case of non-availability of the process. Based on this analysis, appropriate disaster procedures must be developed, and plans should be made. As a part of the disaster recovery, backups of data must be managed at a DR site and be retrievable within the appropriate time frame for system function restoration. In the case of high criticality, real-time mirroring to another site should be deployed.

Key drivers

The key drivers are as followings:

- Natural calamities, like floods or earthquakes
- The primary/main site goes offline due to hardware or software failure
- The system crashes or becomes unresponsive
- The application fails due to non-availability of external systems, networks, or databases

Methodology

This process involves the following key aspects:

- Site level: A DR or redundant site, which is similar to the primary site, can be created to handle natural or unforeseen disasters. This is the normal strategy for disaster recovery (DR) and business continuity. Ensure a DR site is present, which should have a mirror replica of the code and data from the primary site. This serves as a backup site in case of total failure of the primary site. Due to ease of replication and hardware abstraction, the administrators can build the DR environment easily and quickly. Data can be effortlessly synchronized between the primary and DR site using the replication features provided by virtualization.
- DR system should be set up to handle any unforeseen natural disasters. A DR system can also be used as standby nodes to handle additional workload during peak times.
- Backup and recovery: Majority of databases support automatic backup models, that can be configured to back up the data to mirror or backup databases. The standby database cluster in the mirror or backup location would provide seamless failover and recovery capability.
- Data mirroring processes involvs synchronizing the data between the primary site and a remote location, such as a disaster recovery site.
- Disaster recovery and business continuity: This includes the standard set of procedures to be followed, in the event of critical incidents or natural disasters that bring down the entire primary data centre. In order to achieve this, we set up a disaster recovery site, which acts as a failover site for business continuity.

- Recovery using checkpoint and rollback: This technique is mainly leveraged for data intensive systems wherein the software always creates a checkpoint during its consistent or stable state. The application stores its entire state into a persistent storage at regular intervals. During a fault scenario, the fault handler detects the fault and rolls back the application state to the last-known stable checkpoint, which contains a valid, consistent, application state. This technique is widely used in database and operating systems; the same technique is also leveraged for application software. A data-driven application can persist its user session into persistent storage at regular intervals. Each storage will be identified by its timestamp and user credentials. When a user session is corrupted due to incidents or other unforeseen circumstances, the fault handler process can recreate the user session from the previously known valid checkpoint data.

Solution options

The solution options are as follow:

- In the event of an application failure, the organization will be able to failover to a standby site until the primary is back online. The recoverability for the organisation can be planned with backup sites and contingency roadmasp.
- The ability to rollback to a previous state in the event of a major catastrophe or a natural calamity.
- Ability to restore high volume data in the occurrence of corruption or loss. In many organisations, it is vital to be able to roll back to the time just before the incident to avoid painstaking work to recapture the data between the last known good backup and the time of the incident.
- Organisations like to recover beyond the point of the incident.
- Design a store and forward or cached mechanism that allows requests to be stored when the target is offline, and sent when its online.
- Establish ways to identify failures and automatically start the failover process, or route traffic to a spare node.
- Design the solution that uses alternative systems when it detects a number of failed requests to a system.
- Design alternatives to handle non-reliable external systems failed communications and failed transactions.
- Ability to DR must not be compromised by the storage being in the same place as the primary systems.

Checklist

The checklist for the capture or requirements is as follows:

- An organisational disaster management plan has been created that identifies key people, business functions, systems, and processes and put in place mitigations to cope with disaster.
- The system is modifiable, and allows sufficient control to revert to earlier version in the event of failed upgrades
- The data is backed-up at a frequency proportional to the rate of change of data and stored securely and in controlled conditions both offsite (disaster support) and onsite (quick restore)
- The recovery media which includes data, source code, and duplicated hard copy materials is stored in a geographically different location which provides sufficient insulation from regional predicaments whilst still being workable in the event of s natural disaster or incident.
- The recovery media is be stored safely, securely and in controlled conditions
- All mission critical apps have a standby site maintained in an operationally ready state. This site is be capable of replacing the primary site and will be able to provide a hot fail-over capability.
- Key roles are shared between different SMEs to aid recoverability in the case of staff turnover, injury or illness
- An established methodology to test disaster management and recoverability on a periodic basis.

The checklist for architecture definition

- Is a methodology to move from the current environment to the target environment defined?
- Is a migration strategy to transfer the load to the target application defined?
- Has an application backup procedure been identified?
- Does the defined methodology allow reliable restoration of the systems in an acceptable timespan?
- Will the operations team be able to monitor the application landscape in a runtime environment?
- Do the ops team have a clear understanding of the processes they need to perform for the landscape?

- Does the solution takes into account the time taken to recover from system failures?
- Does the backup technique ensure integrity of restored data?
- Does the backup technique support online backups, with acceptable performance degradation?
- Has consideration been given for restoring data from corrupt or incomplete backups states?
- Will the application be able to respond elegantly to errors and exceptions, logging and reporting them into the management and monitoring solution?
- Is a standby site in the DR plan defined? Is the standby site identical to the primary site, or does it offer reduced performance?
- Is the technique for switching from primary to standby site established?
- Have you assessed the impact of the availability solution on functionality and performance? Is this impact acceptable?
- Has the architecture been assessed for single points of failure and other bottlenecks?
- Does the fault-tolerant model extend to all vulnerable components and modules?
- Is the information movement process from the existing environment into the target environment documented?
- Is there an outlined migration strategy to move the workload to the target system?
- How will the landscape deal with data synchronization challenges?
- Has the approach been identified to allow reliable system restoration in an acceptable time spans?
- Does the backup technique provide for integrity of restored data?
- Does the backup technique provide online backup model, with acceptable performance degradation?
- Has attention been given to restoring data from corrupt or incomplete backups?
- Is a standby site defined in the architecture? Is the standby identical to the primary site, or does it offer reduced performance?
- Have you defined and QA'd the technique for swapping from production to standby environments?
- Has the impact of the availability technique on functionality and performance been assessed and is it acceptable?
- Has the architecture been assessed for single points of failure and weaknesses?
- Does your fault-tolerant model extend to all vulnerable entities?

KPIs

The KPI's are as follows:

- Recovery process establishes the **Recovery Point Objectives (RPO)** and **Recovery Time Objectives (RTO)**
- RTO/Restore time: Time required to switch to the secondary site when the primary fails
- RPO/Backup time: Time taken to back up your data
- Backup frequencies: Frequency of backing up the transaction data, config data and code

Interoperability

Interoperability is the ability to exchange information and communicate with internal amd external systems. Interoperable systems make it easier to exchange information both internally and externally. The data formats, transport protocols and interfaces are the key attributes for architecting interoperable systems. Standardization of data formats, transport protocols and interfaces are the key aspects to be considered when architecting interoperable system.

Key drivers

The key drivers are as follows:

- Interaction with legacy or third party systems uses different data exchange formats
- Boundary blurring allows artifacts from one application to defuse into another
- Lack of adherence to standards, frameworks, and best practice

Methodology

There are many ways to establish interoperability in a landscape, but the target is to establish one that is consistently leveraged for the organizations.

This process involves the following key aspects:

- Presentation interoperability is where a common UI approach through a portal-like solution directs the end user to the underlying features.
- Interoperability is sharing the information seamlessly between applications, typically based on common taxnomy, shared services, quality and information security.
- Interoperability is where the functionality is shareable and the applications are seamlessly integrated with an orchestration engine.
- Technical Interoperability consists of techniques for processing, communication, data primarily in the application communications areas. This interoperability deals with rationalization of IT infrastructure, based on standards and common IT framework and platform.

Solution options

The solution options are as follows:

- Consider estabilishing system interoperatibility, while updating separately or even being replaced. For example, leverage orchestration to integrate with legacy or external systems and transform data during exchange.
- Leverage a canonical model for data to manage interactions with different data formats across an enterprise landscape.
- Isolate applications by leveraging interfaces. For example, publish services using interfaces based on standards in order to provide interoperability.
- Architect for high cohesion and low coupling to maximize flexibility and provide plug and play architecture.
- Leverage best practice standards for the domain, rather than creating fresh and proprietary ones.
- Define and publish interfaces including the type and format for communicating.
- Leverage open standards to achieve communication with external applications.
- Publish the semantics of data that is produced and consumed.

Checklist

The checklist for capture of requirements is as follows:

- Each entity can expose a well-defined interface whose syntax and semantics are described for people and other systems to understand.
- Each entity exposes an interoperable interface and does so using common, open, well-documented standards and best practices.
- Each entity that exposes an interoperability interface does so in a way that allows other elements to discover and bind to it. This discovery is facilitated by the use of common, well-documented standards and formats.
- The system includes elements whose sole role is to find, document, manage, bind and orchestrate other systems, and assist with the complexity associated with distributed, service-based, and interoperating elemenst.
- The different types of data produced and consumed are documented in a canonical model and include the relationships between information types.
- The system secures the content of messages passed between systems as they interoperate.
- Exporting information is available in approved formats and standards and includes CSV and XML.

The checklist for architecture definition:

- Are standards, best practice and frameworks leveraged for programming, database approach, nomenclature, user interfaces?
- Is open, consistent and up-to-date technical documentation available?
- Are I/O operations classified in separate modules in order to separate the retrieval of data from the processing of data?
- Is the critical functionality stored in separate modules?
- Are the programs parameterized?
- Are logical values leveraged instead of hard coded values?
- Is it possible to modify input, control, processing and output functions in order to change the way the system works?
- Are the input, output, and processing, implemented separately?
- Are the programs well structured and easy to understand?
- Is the critical functionality contained in distinct modules?

KPIs

The KPI's are as follows:

- Compatibility with shared applications: External applications it needs to integrate with
- Compatibility with external applications: External applications it has to amicably live with
- Different OS compatibilities
- Compatibility with different hardware platforms

Usability

Usability scores characteristics, such as consistency and aesthetics in the user interface. Aesthetics is the visual appearance of the UI. Consistency is the use of techniques employed in the UI. Usability is the ease at which the users operate the application and make productive use of system. Usability is discussed in relation to the system interfaces, but it can just as well be applied to any tool, device, or rich system.

Usability addresses the factors that establish the ability of the software to be understood, used, and learned by its intended users. The application interfaces must be designed with end users in mind so that they are intuitive, are localized, provide access for differently abled users, and provide an excellent customer experience.

Key drivers

The key drivers are as follows:

- Many interactions or excessive clicks are required for tasks
- The incorrect flow of steps in multistep interface
- Data elements and controls are incorrectly structured
- The application is unresponsive or takes a long time to process end-user requests
- Feedback to the user is insufficient, specifically for faults

Methodology

Usability is the ease with which users get the feel of the system and make productive usage of the processes. It is frequently emphazied in relation to the interfaces of the system; it can as well be applied to any device, tool or rich application.

This process involves the following key aspects:

- Efficiency: How efficiently can a end user perform a task once they have learned the UI design
- Learnability: Ease for end users to accomplish primitive processes the first time they encounter the UI.
- Memorability: When users return to the system after a time frame, how quickly can they re-establish expertise
- Errors: How many errors do end users make, how severe are these, and how easily can they recover from these errors?
- Satisfaction: How pleasing is it to use the system

Solution options

The solution options are as follow:

- Design the UI, flows and interaction patterns to maximize ease of use.
- Incorporate workflows to simplify multi-process multi-step operations.
- Design techniques that provide extreme interactivity, such as asynchronous JavaScript, XML (AJAX), and UI validation.
- Leverage asynchronous APIs for long running or background tasks and task populating UI controls.
- Design using appropriate control types such as option groups, check boxes, layout controls, and content using the accepted UI design patterns.
- Identify all touch points where people interact with the application. Know how end users will interact with the application at every touch point.
- Understand capabilities: Experience using computers and interface technologies, the experience within a business function, and the training they will receive.
- Understand the setting in which the application will be leveraged. Is it an internal application that is tightly managed, or exposed to the outside world on a variety of infrastructure?
- Devise an architectural methodology and, where required, a detailed architecture that fits these business requirements.
- QA the architecture against the business requirements.

Checklist

The checklist for the capture of requirements is as follows:

- The overall purpose of the system and the functions is easy to understand for the end users
- Actions are reversible and, where that is not possible, confirmation is clearly sought.
- The system provides an attractive colour scheme and layout. The system is aesthetically pleasing.
- User manuals and guides are complete and up-to-date.
- Context sensitive guidance and help is available for end users.
- The error messages are useful and indicate how to resolve the issue.
- The application provides error messages for validation, verification or runtime problems.
- The system is relatively easy to learn/remember and intuitive for its users.
- The layout, actions, and interface components are consistent.

The checklist for architecture definition

- Ability for an interface to minimise the need for manual keying. For example, information is already contained in system tables which would result in relevant drop-down lists rather than having to type the information in.
- Ability to enable the use of the computer's operational locale (for example, local, regional and resolution settings) in the browser
- Ability to support the multiple browsers: Internet Explorer, Mozilla Firefox, Netscape, Safari.
- Ability to support the different screen resolutions for PC's: (1024x768, 800x600, 1280x1024, 1280x800, 1152x864)
- Ability to support the different delivery channels: PC, Mobile phones, PDA

KPIs

The KPIs are as follows:

- Localization/internationalization requirements cater to languages, spelling, keyboards, paper sizes, and so on
- Look and feel: Screen UI density, layouts and work-flow, colors, metaphors, and keyboard shortcuts.

Summary

This chapter outlined the solutioning part of NFRs, providing insights, guidance and principles for architecting NFRs. This chapter covered all the key NFRs that are critical for any project. For each NFR, it provided the various alternatives pertaining to the solution and design principles that need to be applied to achieve the desired outcome, for example, high availability, scalability, reliability, and so on. The chapter included considerations for bespoke (Java, .NET) and COTS applications and is applicable to IT applications/systems in different domains.

The next chapter outlines the patterns for NFRs, providing insights into architectural patterns and its impact on NFRs. The chapter covers all the key tiers /layers that are critical for any project and describes various patterns pertaining to the business, database and integration tiers. It also covers the impact on various NFRs vis-a-visa the patterns. This chapter will also describe the trade-offs between various NFRs and the best practices to be applied on engagements.

5
Architectural Patterns and its Impact on NFRs

As a software architect or designer, you should be able to read, understand, and apply these models in the context of engagement requirements. One would able to determine if a particular pattern applies to the context in which you are architecting and whether the stated problem exists in your proposed system. You can then follow the pattern and apply it in your particular context.

This is not about a particular technology specification, such as Microsoft's .NET, Oracle's JEE, or a particular product set, such as the Oracle Application Server. This is a conceptual view of systems that we're interested in and how architectural components of the system are arranged. Where appropriate, we have described how a particular technology, platform, or product supports the general concepts. This includes the idea of the relative cost of different solutions since, as a software architect, you will almost certainly become involved in brainstorming at the start of the project cycle when the initial architecture is defined.

This chapter covers the following key topics:

- Patterns and techniques related to architecting NFRs
- Understanding drivers, solutions and the impact on different NFRs
- Metrics, KPIs and methodology for architecting NFRs

Core architecture patterns

This section describes the core architecture patterns and its impact on NFRs:

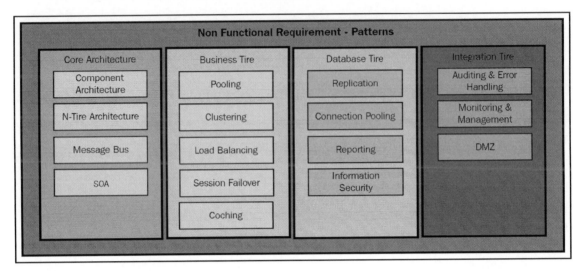

Component-based architecture

To create a good starting point for for a scalable application architecture, a typical system may require a product catalog, registration and personalization, online ordering for the e-commerce domain and various information-based applications, such as a retail outlet finder, and online troubleshooting. Each of these must be logically separated to some degree. As part of the separation, each could be implemented on its own hardware as a set of 'collaborating semi-autonomous applications'. However, they must all combine at different times and in various ways to deliver a 'seamless' experience for the end user.

Context

Creating a business application requires many different types of functionalities, as well as high levels of non-functional characteristics, such as availability, manageability, and performance.

Drivers

Drivers for the component-based architecture solution pattern include:

- Repeated interactions between separate applications can be costly
- Different applications scale at different rates
- Each application will need to be managed separately, which adds greatly to the management overhead of the system
- The interactions between many different applications can create a system that is complex and challenging to maintain
- Different functionality could be delivered by various applications, but each one is then a single point of failure

Solution

Adopt a component-basedarchitecture and group all core system functionality in a single application. Internally partition the application according to the preferred logical architecture. By adopting a collaborating semi-autonomous application architecture, outlined in the previous section, we would end up with a complex architecture consisting of several separate applications. Adopting a component-based architecture means that we lump all this complexity into a single application.

Impact on NFR's

This lists the impact on NFRs of the component-based solution pattern:

NFRs	Description
Availability	The application of this pattern does not in itself improve the availability of the system. However, application server architecture lays the foundation for a highly-available system.
Performance	Performance is likely to be significantly improved. Whereas we had all the semi-autonomous applications collaborating (using some form of inter-process or inter-server communication) to render pages or perform complex functions, now we have a single application, although parts of this may still require inter-process communication, depending on implementation choices.

Scalability	The application of this pattern does not in itself improve the scalability of the system. However, application server architecture lays the foundation for a highly scalable system.
Security	Security is marginally improved due to having only one application and one database to worry about securing.
Manageability	Manageability is significantly improved: as earlier we had many applications to manage, now we only have one. Even when we add more complexity to the architecture to achieve scalability, and so on. Application server architecture lays the foundation for a more manageable system.
Maintainability	Because all the logically separate software 'modules' are part of the same application, we don't have to worry about complex communication mechanisms. However, we have not lost the benefits of having well-defined sets of functionality which can, potentially, help to isolate bugs. On the whole, maintainability is improved.
Flexibility	This type of system architecture is flexible as we have a partitioning, which gives us flexibility.
Portability	Not affected.
Cost	Application server architecture provides a foundation where manageability, performance, availability, and scalability can be addressed more easily (and therefore more cheaply). Running the application in the .NET framework or on a JEE application server can potentially reduce costs; the cost of purchasing the infrastructure can easily be offset by the cost of building all the functionality provided from scratch.

N-tier architecture

Independently scale, tune and improve the availability of the web and application architecture. Good performance is a key requirement in order to make such a system usable.

Context

We have web and application servers that perform different tasks. However, if these servers are deployed on the same hardware, the hardware cannot be tuned or scaled for the individual types of server. They are lumped together leading to sub-optimal performance and increased licensing and configuration costs.

Drivers

Drivers for an n-tier architecture solution pattern include:

- The web and application servers will usually scale at different rates, with the web server being able to handle more concurrent users than the application server.
- If the web and application servers are bound together, failure of a web server will result in no requests being delivered to the associated application server.
- Application server software licenses tend to cost more money than web server software, and these licenses are usually on a per processor basis, so more hardware servers running the application server will cost more money regardless of whether that capacity is used or not.
- It is hard to optimize a hardware server for both memory-intensive computation and disk or network I/O.
- Only a small amount of the response returned to the user may involve application server functionality.

Solution

Deploy the web server and application server software onto dedicated hardware servers that are optimized to support these different types of functionality. Architecture introduces separate tiers of web and application servers. Both are deployed as load-balanced elements.

The split between web and application servers is generally carried out on both the hardware and software elements. This means that both hardware and software can be tuned for the web and application server functions.

Impact on NFRs

This lists the impacts on NFRs of the n-tier architecture solution pattern.

NFRs	Description
Availability	Availability is improved due to the separation of the web servers from the rest of the system software: a web server can fail without having an adverse impact on any particular application software instance.
Performance	Performance can be improved depending on the degree to which the web and application/data hardware servers can be optimized. This relies on the type of application and its interface: sites with lots of graphics or large binary assets to be downloaded, or particularly complex application functionality, are likely to benefit most from the split.
Scalability	Scalability is improved due to the ability to scale the web server and application server load-balanced pools independently.
Security	Security is negatively impacted as there are now a number of new elements that need to be secured. However, dedicated web and application servers does provide the foundation for the demilitarized zone security pattern.
Manageability	Manageability is negatively impacted due to the need to separately manage the web servers and application servers, plus the additional load balancers.
Maintainability	Maintainability is potentially improved as problems unique to the web servers can be isolated on those machines. Equally, the web servers and the application server stack can be fixed independently if necessary.
Flexibility	Not affected.
Portability	Not affected.
Cost	The introduction of a number of new hardware servers may initially have a negative impact on cost, depending on the size of the servers required. However, the use of optimized or specialist hardware should prove cheaper in the long run: scaling the system doesn't necessarily require new hardware of all types to be purchased.

Message Bus

A Message Bus pattern describes the principle of using a system that can send and receive messages using one or more communication channel, so that applications can interact without knowing details about one another. This a design methodology where interaction between applications is accomplished by passing asynchronous messages over the bus. Common Message Bus leverage architecture either leverage a messaging router, or use a publish and subscribe pattern, and are implemented using a messaging system such as a queue. Many Message Bus implementations consist of individual applications communicating using predefined schema and a shared infrastructure for sending and receiving messages.

Context

Message Bus designs are leveraged to support complex processing for many organizations. This design provides a pluggable architecture that allows you to integrate applications into the main business processes, or improve scalability by attaching several instances of the application to the Message Bus. Variations on Message Bus pattern include:

- **Enterprise Service Bus (ESB)**: Based on the designs, an ESB leverages services for communication between the bus and applications attached to this Message Bus. ESB provides services that transform messages from one format to another, allowing an applications that use incompatible message formats to communicate with one another.
- **Cloud Service Bus (ISB)**: Similar to a Message Bus, but the main bus infrastructure is hosted in the cloud instead of in the company data center. A core methodology is the use of **Uniform Resource Identifiers** (**URIs**) and policies to control the routing mechanism through applications and services in the cloud.

Drivers

Drivers for the Message Bus solution pattern include:

- **Low complexity**: Complexity is reduced because each application only communicates with the bus, and the bus, in turn, is integrated with the other endpoint applications
- **Extensibility**: Applications can be added to or removed from the Message Bus without impacting the existing architecture.

- **Loose coupling**: As long as applications expose interfaces via the Message Bus, there is no dependency on the application, allowing updates, changes, and replacements.
- **Flexibility**: The set of applications that make up the entire organizational landscape can be easily changed to fit changes in business requirements, simply through changes in the configuration or parameters.
- **Simplicity**: Although the Message Bus component adds complexity to the architecture, each application is required to support only one connection to the bus instead of multiple connections to other applications in the landscape.
- **Scalability**: Multiple instances of the application may be attached to the bus in order to handle increased workload.

Solution

This pattern is applicable if you are architecting a solution that requires integration with external applications, or applications hosted in different environments. This is also the appropriate pattern if you have existing applications that interoperate with each other, or you want to combine multiple processes into a single workflow.

This pattern applies software elements.

Impact on NFRs

This lists the impact on NFRs of the Message Bus solution pattern:

NFRs	Description
Availability	On the whole, the availability of the core application is improved due to the Message Bus architecture. If the peripheral application fails, the core application can continue to function.
Performance	Overall system performance is potentially improved. The performance of the applications will also be improved if they are hosted on their own dedicated hardware rather than sharing with the core application.
Scalability	The scalability of the overall system is largely unaltered, but the separation of extraordinary functionality allows it to be scaled independently from the core system elements.
Security	As it introduces more and different elements into the system, can make security more of a challenge. However, by separating these elements security can be individually tailored.

Manageability	Manageability of the functionality is improved because each specialist application can be managed appropriately. However, manageability of the system as a whole is negatively impacted because different management procedures and techniques have to be introduced for each application.
Maintainability	The use of a Message Bus improves the maintainability of the system as any problem with the specialist functionality is isolated in its own application.
Flexibility	Message Bus frequently delivers additional, non-core, functionality in a flexible manner and hence additional applications can be plugged into the architecture
Portability	Portability is largely not affected when we consider the Message Bus and the bespoke applications. Unless we choose to implement them in different technologies, porting the core Message Bus and business application is likely to be as easy or as difficult as porting one application with both core and specialist functionality.
Cost	Choosing the specialist behavior like this will increase our costs: we will increase the number of hardware servers, and we have increased our maintainability problem (a primary source of ongoing cost).

Service-oriented architecture

Service-oriented architecture (SOA) allows functionality to be provided as a set of services and by the creatiion of applications that leverage services. Services are loosely coupled components as they use standards-based APIs that can be published, invoked, and discovered. SOA services are focused on providing schema and message-based integrations through application interfaces, and are not component or object-based. An SOA service should not be treated as a component-based service provider.

Context

SOA patterns package business processes into interoperable services, using different data formats and protocols to communicate information. Clients and other services can access services running on the same tier or remote services over a network.

Drivers

Drivers for the SOA solution pattern include:

- SOA is the preferred choice for application integration with internal and external systems. For most of the enterprise integrations, a light weight services integration is preferred.
- Popular use of service is in the form of REST/SOAP-based services used in web architecture. All the utility components that are needed by external or third party applications can be exposed as web services.
- Legacy applications and ERP systems also provide a service interface as an integration option with enterprise applications.

Solution

SOA involves exposing modular and independent functions as services so that the service consumer can re-use and build a larger application functionality. Best practice for building services is that they should be reusable, stateless, loosely coupled, and granular and should abstract the inner application logic. SOA is the most popular pattern used in enterprises for applications integration. Key building blocks of SOA are a service provider, service consumer, **Universal Description and Discovery Integration (UDDI)** registry, and the **Web Services Description Language (WSDL)** file containing the service definition.

This pattern applies software elements.

Impact on NFRs

The following lists the impact on NFRs of the SOA solution pattern:

NFRs	Description
Availability	On the whole, the availability of the application is improved due to splitting in services.
Performance	Overall system performance is potentially improved. The performance of the services will also be enhanced if they are hosted on their own dedicated hardware rather than sharing with the core application.

Scalability	As services are mostly stateless and promote loose coupling, it enables the scalability of both service provider and service consumer. SOA also enables architects to leverage scalability-friendly features such as invoking services on-demand, asynchronous service invocation, light-weight data transfer, and so on. SOA allows reuse of modules and components which help in achieving integration scalability.
Security	As it introduces more and different elements into the system, it can make security more of a challenge. However, by using the security controls their security can be individually tailored.
Manageability	Manageability of the functionality is improved because each service element can be managed appropriately.
Maintainability	The use of service elements can improve the maintainability of the system as any problem with the service elements is isolated in its own context.
Flexibility	SOA can deliver additional, non-core, functionality in a flexible manner.
Portability	Portability is widely improved. Even if we choose to implement them in different technologies, porting the application is likely to be as easy. Choosing to implement functionality using off-the-shelf products (commercial or non-commercial) can affect portability.
Cost	On the face of it, choosing SOA like this will increase our costs: we will probably increase the number of hardware servers, and we have increased our maintainability problem (a primary source of ongoing cost). However, we have to trade this off against potential savings: use of off-the-shelf products (commercial or non-commercial) can save money compared to developing the functionality ourselves.

Business tier patterns

This section describes the business tier solution patterns and their impact on NFRs.

Active/Passive clustering

This pattern warrants that the system as a whole continues to function if part(s) of the system go offline.

Context

Architecting an n-tier architecture where high availability is one of the prime non-functional requirements.

Drivers

Drivers for the active/passive solution pattern include:

- The system has a required level of availability which must be delivered even in the face of hardware or software failure.
- The system has to be maintained and upgraded over time. Even with planned downtime, there may be a need to upgrade or fix a system element whilst ensuring the system remains available.

Solution

Provide alternative capacity for your critical system elements by duplicating those elements. Redirect users to the duplicate should the active element become unavailable.

This pattern must be applied equally to hardware and software. Software elements are, perhaps, more prone to failure than hardware because they are inherently more complex. They are also likely to be the elements that need to be taken out of service for maintenance (usually to have their functionality upgraded). However, this isn't to say that hardware is immune to failure or requires no maintenance. And there is no point having a single hardware element running an active-redundant pair of software elements. If the hardware fails, the system is down. Architecture introduces redundant switches and servers that will automatically swap in should the active one fail.

Impact on NFRs

The following table lists the impact on NFRs of the active/passive solution pattern:

NFRs	Description
Availability	Availability of the system is improved due to the presence of a redundant element that can take over in the event that an active element fails or has to be taken out of service for maintenance.

Performance	There will be a minuscule (possibly insignificant) negative impact on performance due to the introduction of the 'failover' mechanism that switches in the redundant element should the active one fail.
Scalability	Not affected.
Security	Security may be negatively impacted by the additional element and failover mechanism, both of which have to be secured.
Manageability	Manageability is negatively impacted as part has been replaced by two and the failover mechanism also has to be managed.
Maintainability	Not affected.
Flexibility	Not affected.
Portability	Not affected.
Cost	The impact on cost can be significant: where there was a single element, there are now two (plus the cost of implementing the failover mechanism). If the elements are identical, we have basically doubled the cost of introducing that element. We can mitigate this by introducing a cheaper version of the element as the redundant one, but this restricts our implementation choices: we would definitely want to switch back to the active element as soon as it is introduced back into service.

Load-balancing architecture

To ensure the system continues to function when elements become unavailable and when system load increases beyond the capacity of a single element.

Context

Architecting an enterprise-level system where high availability is one of the prime non-functional requirements. In active/passive clustering there is a reduction in performance and scalability when a lower-capacity redundant element is in service, and the cost of having full-capacity redundant elements is too high.

Drivers

Drivers for the load-balancing architecture solution pattern include:

- The system has a required level of availability which must be delivered even in the face of hardware or software failure.
- The system has to be maintained and upgraded over time. Even with planned downtime, there may be a need to upgrade or fix a system element whilst ensuring the system remains available.
- When implementing active/passive elements, the number of users accessing a reduced capacity redundant server can be restricted to a level matching its capabilities. However, this will effectively make the server unavailable to the remaining users, which may not be satisfactory.
- Specifying a redundant server to the same level as that of the active server means that there will be no degradation in performance, but is economically unacceptable for most organizations.
- The system has a required level of performance in the face of a particular user load which it needs to maintain even though hardware and software elements will be taken out of service due to failure or the need for maintenance.
- The system will need to deliver a consistent level of performance in the face of increased user load. There must be some way of increasing the system capacity should this load exceed original estimates.

Solution

Use multiple elements of similar capability and balance the load continuously across them to achieve the required throughput and response. To increase capacity, add further elements to the load-balanced set.

Both software and hardware load balancers are available. The actual load balancing tends to be across software elements, with the load balancing across hardware achieved as a consequence of the software elements running on that hardware.

Impact on NFRs

This lists the impact on NFRs of the load-balancing architecture solution pattern:

NFRs	Description
Availability	Availability is improved. As with active/passive elements, loss of an element due to failure or maintenance does not mean the system ceases to function. In cases where we would have a much lower capacity redundant element for reasons of cost, load-balanced elements are likely to provide better capacity. Unlike active/passive elements, load-balanced elements can also cope with multiple failures or failure during maintenance.
Performance	Performance is negatively impacted as the load balancer needs to determine the element to which it should forward a request.
Scalability	Scalability is greatly improved. With active/passive elements, we can only scale the system by increasing the capacity of the active element (possibly only by replacing it). Using load-balanced elements, we can increase the capacity of the system by adding new elements to the load-balanced set. The load balancer will ensure they receive their 'fair share' of requests, and the system is scaled.
Security	Security is negatively impacted due to the introduction of additional elements that need to be protected.
Manageability	There is a great negative impact on manageability. We now have a number of additional elements to manage, and that number can grow according to our scalability needs.
Maintainability	Not affected.
Flexibility	Not affected.
Portability	Not affected.
Cost	Cost may not be too severely impacted. Depending on the type of hardware, the cost of buying a large number of medium-capacity servers may be lower than the cost of buying one high-capacity and one low capacity (redundant) server. This could be a bit more expensive, but it is rare that it is a lot more expensive. The cost of the load balancer needs to be added to the expense of the system.

Session failover

To ensure the system continues to function by preserving the session state in the event of server failure.

Context

The system maintains an interaction state in the form of a user session held on the server. The system maintains extensive in-memory state, for example, a customer order. The client's order state is kept in memory until the customer submits the order. The process of assembling an order may take any length of time from a couple of minutes up to several hours.

Drivers

Drivers for the session failover solution pattern include:

- Failures in software or hardware may well occur while the user is in the middle of interacting with the system, but we cannot allow that failure to interrupt the user's interaction or the server to lose valuable data.
- Having either a redundant or load-balanced, functionally-identical element that can take over from a failed element means that the user can continue interacting with the system, but that element needs to be able to get at the state of the user's interaction with the user to be able to continue that interaction uninterrupted.
- Storing the state information either as part of the request URL or one or more cookies means that any element involved in fulfilling the request can get the information, but the nature of the interaction means the amount and sensitivity of the information make this choice inappropriate.

Solution

Implement a mechanism that holds session information whilst the user is interacting with the system and makes this information available to the duplicate servers in the system.

Architecture introduces a session persistence mechanism in the form of a session backup server. The session state is saved whenever it is changed in response to a request. We introduce request-based failover so that the system software tries to load session state from the session backup server whenever it receives a request that forms part of a session that it doesn't recognize.

This pattern applies essentially to software. The state is maintained in the context of a software component, and the session backup server is usually implemented in software. Hardware is only required to host the backup server--sometimes this hosting is provided by a dedicated hardware server, sometimes the backup servers live on the same hardware server as the system software.

Impact on NFRs

This lists the impact of NFRs of the session failover solution pattern:

NFRs	Description
Availability	Availability is improved as the user's session state is maintained even if the requests need to be directed to a new server due to the loss of the one that had been maintaining that state.
Performance	Performance is likely to be negatively impacted due to the need to save the user's session state periodically.
Scalability	Not affected.
Security	We have introduced some new system elements--the session backup server and its redundant pair, that need to be secured. We also have a mechanism that saves the state information. We have to ensure that sensitive information is not stored as part of the state or is obscured in some way
Manageability	Manageability is negatively impacted due to the introduction of a new mechanism and associated elements that all have to be managed.
Maintainability	Maintainability can be marginally improved as it is possible to retrieve information about the state of user sessions in the event of system failure.
Flexibility	Not affected.
Portability	Not affected.
Cost	The cost is most likely to be affected by whether dedicated session backup servers (both software and hardware elements) are purchased. This maximizes availability but incurs significant expense.

Resource pooling

Maximize the utilization of expensive resources.

Context

Architecture needs to provide resources to processes or threads that are expensive to initialize and implementing connection pooling optimizes the use of these resources.

Drivers

Drivers for the resource pooling solution pattern include:

- We want to maximize overall system performance (throughput) by limiting connections, but we also want to maximize individual user performance (end-to-end).
- It is not usually financially justifiable to specify enough capacity for inexpensive resources for each projected user of the system.
- Resource usage tends to vary over the course of a request. Not all resources are required for the whole lifetime of the request.
- Obtaining and initializing resources are typically expensive in terms of time and processing power. This initialization should be avoided where possible.

Solution

Implement a pool of resources from which it is relatively inexpensive to acquire such resources and to which they can quickly be released when no longer required. Each of the application servers has a pool of connections that it uses to connect to the database server cluster. The pool is limited in size by licensing constraints. The business components will obtain a database connection just before they need it and release it as soon as they have finished with it.

This pattern applies to both hardware and software.

Impact on NFRs

This lists the impact on NFRs of the resource pooling solution pattern:

NFRs	Description
Availability	Not affected
Performance	Performance is improved due to the reuse of limited resources that can be expensive to create or initialize

Scalability	Sharing of valuable resources enables more users to connect to the system than otherwise
Security	Not affected
Manageability	There is a slightly negative impact on manageability due to the need to manage the resource pool
Maintainability	Not affected
Flexibility	Not affected
Portability	Not affected
Cost	Many products support resource pooling as standard, and bespoke implementation is not a significant investment

Caching

Speeding up access to information distributed across multiple servers

Context

The application database is housed on its own hardware server. This introduces a performance problem as all queries, and resultant data have to travel over the network connection between each application instance and the database.

Drivers

Drivers for the caching solution pattern include:

- A common persistent store ensures information integrity, but this means that all system elements have to compete for the resource, potentially introducing a bottleneck.
- A distributed architecture with a common persistent store gives advantages in reliability and robustness but means that data access has to be inter rather than intra-process.
- Data integrity is of prime importance, but much data is slow-changing, and a system element may read the same piece of data many times before it changes.

Solution

Identify information that changes infrequently compared to the frequency with which it is accessed and cache it locally to where it is used. Each of the application servers caches data that it reads from the DBMS. When this information is next required by an application component, it can be retrieved from the local cache without reference to the database.

This pattern applies to both hardware and software.

Impact on NFRs

This lists the impact on NFRs of the caching solution pattern:

NFRs	Description
Availability	Potentially there is a minor improvement in availability. If the common persistent store fails, some data is still available in the local cache. However, only a subset of functionality is likely to remain available; functions such as ordering require access to the persistent store, not merely to a cache.
Performance	Performance is improved by the local availability of data or assets that would otherwise have to be retrieved from a remote store.
Scalability	Not affected.
Security	We need to consider the type of information being held in the local cache. If the information is sensitive, the introduction of the cache has an adverse impact on security as we have to protect the cache as well as the persistent store.
Manageability	There is a negative impact on manageability as we have to manage the cache and any caching parameters that can be 'tuned'.
Maintainability	Not affected.
Flexibility	Not affected.
Portability	Not affected.
Cost	The cost of implementing a local cache depends on its sophistication. It is relatively easy to build and maintain a very simple cache, and the cost is minimal. However, an adaptive cache that holds frequently updated information is harder to build and products that perform this function can be expensive to buy.

Database tier patterns

This section describes the database tier patterns and its impact on NFRs.

Data replication

To deliver high availability, we must introduce some level of duplication of system elements. However, if those elements store data, no inconsistency can be tolerated between them.

Context

Read-only data, such as report data, computed results so on, can be replicated to multiple database instances so as to enable parallel reads. Most databases support automatic data replication and data synchronization features, which can also be leveraged. Data replication is often carried out by a master-slave configuration either synchronously or asynchronously. Replication jobs should be configured to optimize throughput and latency.

Drivers

Drivers for the data replication solution pattern include:

- We need a common persistent store to ensure a consistent view of the system across all application servers (whether active-redundant or load-balanced).
- High availability architectures depend on application data and code. Hence it is essential to have high availability for data and code. One of the popular strategies is site replication which is also used to handle DR.
- The database objects, schema updates, and data will be replicated to all mirror sites by the synchronization job. For optimization, only the incremental/differential data will be chosen for synchronization.

Solution

This section describes master slave and DR configurations.

Master-slave configuration: Replication requires multiple copies of data to be dispersed across different databases. In such a setup, the read-only operations will be faster and scalable as it is possible to read from the nearest database instance and it can answer a number of read-only queries in parallel.

DR configuration: This involves copying the data from the primary instance to all its backup and standby instances so that it is easy to switch in case of failover. Replication is a practice followed by storage systems, database servers, and in cases of application configurations.

The two main types of replication configuration are:

- **Active replication:** In this configuration, the request from the client is processed by all instances. This configuration is used for real-time systems.
- **Passive replication:** In this configuration, the primary node processes the request, and it is then copied over to secondary nodes.

This pattern is usually implemented in software, often as part of the database management system. Additional hardware is introduced to give tolerance to both hardware and software failure and maintenance.

Impact on NFRs

This describes the impact on NFRs of the data replication solution pattern:

NFRs	Description
Availability	Availability is improved by replacing the single point of failure with a pair of active/passive elements.
Performance	There is a significant negative impact on performance for any operation that involves writing data to the database.
Scalability	Scalability is improved as due to reading only and database setup.
Security	As long as the security mechanisms work in the same way for a pair of active/passive elements as they do on a single server, security is not affected.
Manageability	Manageability will be negatively impacted due to the need to manage the active-redundant pair of elements and the data replication mechanism.

Maintainability	Maintainability should be unaffected unless there are problems with the data replication mechanism itself, in which case there could be uncertainty as to the state of the data set the application is using
Flexibility	Not affected.
Portability	Data replication is often implemented using proprietary mechanisms that have their own non-functional characteristics. If the database is accessed using SQL, potentially it can be swapped with another SQL--compliant database, but the new database may not have a data replication mechanism, or it might work in a very different way.
Cost	The simplest way to implement such a complex mechanism as data replication is to buy a persistent storage product that supports it. This can be very expensive, particularly when compared with other products that don't support data replication but otherwise meet all the functional and non-functional requirements for the system. Bespoke solutions can be developed, but these are usually reasonably complex and take time and money to establish and maintain.

Connection pooling

By using connection pooling in an instance where there are more users than we can service degrading the service performance, one can efficiently manage the database connections through reusability and so it can be easily scaled.

Context

We have a set of web servers that we believe can comfortably handle simultaneous users. However, we only have enough application instances to serve simultaneous users. We have the option of adding more servers to scale the application, but this will be costly, and we don't see it as being necessary at the moment. However, suppose something unexpected happens, and more than the usual number of users all turn up at the same time: the web servers will cope, but the application servers will struggle, and everyone will experience poor performance.

Drivers

Drivers for the connection pooling solution pattern include:

- We want to serve as many users as possible, but we also want to make sure that each individual user has a good experience. Having many users accessing a constrained resource at the same time will give a proportionately slower experience.
- It is usually not financially justifiable to specify each element of the system to meet the anticipated peak load. Even if you do, sudden spikes could possibly exceed this peak and degrade performance.

Solution

This involves creating a managed pool of resources which would be costly to establish and maintain in real time. A thread pool, database connection pool, and service pool would offer great flexibility in scaling the applications during peak load. The pool architecture offers many features, such as initial connections, minimum/maximum pool connections, maximum time-out, and idle time-out values.

Resource pools such as database connection pools also maintain multiple logical connections over fewer physical connections, and they also reuse the connections, which bring in more scalability to the applications.

Establishing and maintaining a connection with external resources, such as databases and service endpoints, are costly operations. They consume a lot of critical resources such as CPU and memory. Using-managed resource pools allow for optimally maintaining the connections with minimal system overhead. The decreased overhead on system resources, such as CPU and memory, increase capability. An important principle of resource pooling is that they can handle a higher number of resource requests by efficiently managing the pools and hence are providing excellent application scalability.

This pattern applies to both software and hardware.

Impact on NFRs

This describes the impact on NFRs of the connection pooling solution pattern:

NFRs	Description
Availability	Availability will improve as we will be able to service more users with limited numbers of resources using pooling.

Performance	We can guarantee a level of performance regardless of the demand for the system.
Scalability	Scalability is improvedScalability is improved by limiting the number of connections to the system. The view on scalability is that it defines the system's ability to cope with increased load without degrading performance significantly. By imposing connection pooling patterns, we can ensure good scalability up to that limit and then prevent degradation due to overloading.
Security	Not affected.
Manageability	There is a slightly negative impact on manageability due to the need to manage the connection limit.
Maintainability	Not affected.
Flexibility	Not affected.
Portability	Not affected.
Cost	The cost of implementing a connection limit is low. A number of products support this concept as standard, but even a bespoke implementation is not that big a job.

Reporting

To extract valuable information from a system without significantly impacting the ability of that system to do its job.

Context

We have implemented a high-capability system that gathers data as it processes user transactions. This data contains useful business information about those transactions, including who performed the transaction, when it took place, how it related to other transactions and how the system behaved during the transaction. By performing proper analysis on this data, the business can detect trends, for example, product sales and customer demographics. The operations team can also use such data to predict system load and detect potential overload. The system gathers information such as orders placed, duration of transactions, and page views. This information can be analyzed to determine which products were commonly bought together. This can be further refined when it is split on a demographic basis (for example, retailers who are identified as operating in a higher-income area).

There may be many such analyses that are required--some standard and some ad hoc--as the business tries to determine the best combination of offers and marketing to suit the needs of its customers. Using live system data as the basis for such analyses puts an additional, intensive load on the system database and degrades the performance of the system

Drivers

Drivers for the reporting solution pattern include:

- Lots of intensive data processing is required to create useful reports, but such processing slows down the live system.
- Reporting tends to be historical and/or predictive. In either case, the data does not need to be completely up-to-the-minute.
- Users of the reporting mechanisms are internal to the organization, while the main application is focused on delivering information to external users.
- Users of the reporting mechanisms are inside the internal firewall. Providing access to specific parts of the external system will require a more complex firewall configuration.
- If a report is generated from live system data, all of the updates from a (long running) business transaction may not have been applied when the report is generated, potentially giving misleading results.
- *Ad hoc* reports generated in real-time may be required against the data.
- For a simple system, it would be possible to minimize such contention by running reports 'overnight', that is, at a time of low system load. For systems that are used 24×7, there may be no ideal timeslot at which user load is sufficiently low that running a big report would not impact system responsiveness.

Solution

Periodically the snapshot data is required for analysis. The snapshot of data is exported from live system environment so that any reporting can be carried out offline.

The queries required to generate the snapshots will have an impact on the database, but nowhere near as big an impact as running the reporting against it. We can also parameterize the snapshot mechanisms as much as we like, for example, by specifying that we're only interested in how users view certain areas of the site or the profiles of new customers.

This pattern applies only to software.

Impact on NFRs

This describes the impact on the NFRs of the reporting solution pattern:

NFRs	Description
Availability	Not affected.
Performance	Performance is improved as we have isolated an essential but 'expensive' process from the live system.
Scalability	Not affected.
Security	Security is potentially negatively impacted as we create snapshots of possibly sensitive data. These snapshots need to be protected from anyone who should not have access to them. One has to be cautious that the export mechanism does not leave security holes that may be hacked to gain access to the corporate environment.
Manageability	Manageability is negatively impacted due to the introduction of new mechanisms and system access points that have to be managed.
Maintainability	Not affected.
Flexibility	Not affected.
Portability	Not affected.
Cost	The implementation cost really depends on the sophistication of the snapshot and export mechanisms. If we don't mind exporting the whole database in a single, un-parameterized snapshot and the database product supports snapshots being taken whilst it is still running, this should be a straightforward and cheap mechanism to implement. If we want to be more selective about what we snapshot and how we export it, we will need to build a bespoke solution, which could be reasonably expensive to build and maintain.

Information security

To ensure that sensitive data gathered and stored by the system is protected from unauthorized access

Context

The application gathers customer data as part of its normal operation. The system holds a variety of configuration information that could be of use to a potential attacker. The application is exposed to an environment which contains potential attackers. Applications manipulate a lot of information some of which is sensitive, such as credit card details. A cracker breaching the system should not find it easy to discover this information and make use of it for commercial gain or fraudulent purposes.

Drivers

Drivers for the information security solution pattern include:

- Data needs to be accessible by different parts of the system but should not be easily viewable by potential intruders.
- Encryption and decryption are comparatively slow and expensive (in resource terms) and so should be avoided unless necessary.
- Much data is non-sensitive in nature and does not need protecting.
- The level of encryption used should be weighed against the likelihood of unauthorized access to the data.

Solution

Grade the information held by the system for sensitivity. Encrypt the most sensitive items of data using encryption and obfuscation techniques. All *public* data, such as catalog information held in caches and in memory on the web servers is held in plain text. However, credit card details are held in encrypted form. The only place in the system that such details appear in plain text is in memory on the application server as it is delivering this information, for example, the credit card processing agency.

This pattern mainly applies to software, although hardware acceleration may be used.

Impact on NFRs

This describes the impact on NFRs of the information security solution pattern:

NFRs	Description
Availability	Availability should not be negatively impacted, but care should be taken not to introduce single points of failure in the form of encryption key distribution and management services.
Performance	Performance is negatively impacted if an obscurity mechanism is introduced, because of the processing overhead associated with the mechanism. This applies in particular to complex encryption algorithms with long key lengths.
Scalability	There should not be a negative impact on scalability, but any mechanisms used by the security policy, such as encryption key distribution and management services, should themselves be scalable.
Security	Security is improved by data obscurity because, even in the event of an attack during which the attacker may gain access to the file system, system memory, and application database, any sensitive data is not usable by the attacker. Security is also improved by configuration obscurity as any attacker will find it harder to obtain the information they need to crack the system.
Manageability	Manageability is negatively impacted as additional resources will be needed for the encryption mechanism (such as key management).
Maintainability	Obfuscation techniques, in particular, can affect the maintainability of the system as the developers have to remember obscure names for the configuration files, and so on.
Flexibility	Flexibility may be negatively impacted as you may need to maintain back-compatibility with existing encrypted data or obscured configuration.
Portability	Portability is negatively impacted as you must ensure that any new platform supports the encryption mechanisms you wish to use.
Cost	Cost is probably increased due to the additional requirements of encryption which may require either additional capability to support software encryption or dedicated encryption hardware. One may need to buy additional encryption software depending on the capabilities of the existing platforms and tools.

Integration tier patterns

This section describes the integration tier patterns and its impact on NFRs.

Logging and exception management

To control your system effectively you need to be armed with information at regular intervals about what each system element is doing.

Context

The system has stringent requirements for performance, scalability, and availability. The failure of any system element could potentially impact the level of capability in these areas. In order to prevent system crashes or predict when new capacity is needed, you must have some current and historical data on system usage.

The web servers, application servers, and database servers (both hardware and software) all play vital roles in the system. If one of the web servers fails, the load on the other web servers increases. This could lead to poor performance for the users or even to the failure of one of the remaining web servers. This sequence of events may well go unnoticed unless you can determine the health and capacity of the web servers.

Drivers

Driver for the logging and exception management solution pattern include:

- When the application is deployed into the live, staging, or test environments, operational, security, and practical considerations mitigate against the use of standard development techniques (such as debugging) to examine the internal state of the system.
- Web applications are subject to huge and unpredictable variations in their use. This makes it difficult to decide which system elements we need status information from and what degree of information is necessary.

- Monitoring every system element involves more effort (cost) to set up, degrades performance, and reduces manageability due to the increased data generated. Every element has a vital role to play and, consequently, can significantly affect the overall health of the system if it fails or is subject to excessive load.

- Generating lots of information from a system element involves more effort (cost) to set up, degrades performance and reduces manageability due to the increased data generated. The amount and type of information required depends on the purpose for which the information is used. Restricting the information generated may prevent the correct diagnosis of problems.

- It may be cheaper and more manageable to have system elements store status information about them and analyze that information off-line. This does give us the ability to react immediately to changes that might threaten the health of the system.

Solution

Define a reporting interface or protocol for every type of system element that can seriously affect the health of the overall system. Have each individual system element continuously report its status according to its type. Log some or all of the data generated so that it is available for subsequent offline analysis.

We add status reporting capability to the web servers, application servers, and data access servers. Using a variety of reporting techniques, including the SNMP protocol, each of the components reports its use of limited resources such as memory, CPU, and disk space (all); sockets (web servers); database connections (application servers); and cursors (data access servers). The type and amount of information generates the frequency of generation and the protocol used to export it depends on the requirements of any monitoring, alerting or prediction systems that use it.

Reporting must be performed by virtually every system element regardless of whether it is hardware or software. For simple elements such as a hardware switch, the status information may be as simple as an indicator that it is still functioning. For more complex elements such as the hardware database server, there may be a significant amount of highly-detailed information.

Impact on NFRs

This table describes the impact on NFRs of the logging and exception management solution pattern:

NFRs	Description
Availability	Availability is potentially improved as the generated information can be used to identify and predict element failure or overload.
Performance	Performance is negatively impacted because of the overhead of the continuous reporting.
Scalability	Not affected.
Security	There is potentially a negative impact on the security as extended system information is available to any intruder who has the capability of monitoring network traffic.
Manageability	Manageability is improved because up-to-date information about each element's condition is continuously available.
Maintainability	Maintainability is potentially improved because management information can sometimes be useful in diagnosing a fault or problem. For example, requests for dynamic pages failing when the data access servers take more than 30 seconds to pass back the result set may indicate a predefined time-out in the database drivers used by the application servers.
Flexibility	Not affected.
Portability	Not affected.
Cost	The cost of introducing continuous reporting for every type of system element is always going to be significant whether the element supports reporting out of the box or not. This cost is justified because continuous status reporting is at the heart of a controllable system.

Enterprise Monitoring and Management

This section describes the enterprise monitoring and management patterns and its impact on NFRs. To allow operators to spot potential problems in the large volume of information generated by status reporting from complex or high-volume application. To control your system effectively you need to be armed with information at regular intervals about what each system element is doing.

Context

We have an n-tier architecture that uses a number of different hardware and software servers. The system has stringent requirements for performance, scalability, and availability. The failure of any system element could potentially impact the level of capability in these areas. In order to prevent system crashes or predict when new capacity is needed, we must have some current and historical data on system usage.

Drivers

Drivers for the enterprise monitoring and management solution patterns include:

- Applications are subject to enormous and unpredictable variations in their use. This makes it difficult to decide which system elements we need status information from and what degree of information is necessary.

- When the application is deployed into live, staging or test environments, operational, security and practical considerations mitigate against the use of standard development techniques (such as debugging) to examine the internal state of the system.

- To reduce cost and simplify procedures, we will need to restrict the number of people on the system operations team. However, many parameters can indicate immediate or potential problems in a system, and a large amount of generated data becomes increasingly difficult for a limited system operations team to process manually in a timely fashion (that is, soon enough to avert system failure).

- Monitoring all of the system elements is costly (in terms of time at least) and will impact performance and manageability due to the amount of data generated. Every element has a vital role to play and, consequently, can significantly affect the overall health of the system if it fails or is subject to excessive load.

- Generating lots of information from a system element involves more effort (cost) to set up, degrades performance and reduces manageability due to the increased data generated. The amount and type of information required depends on the purpose for which the information is used. Restricting the information generated may prevent the correct diagnosis of problems.

- It may be cheaper and more manageable to have system elements store status information about them and analyze that information off-line or at set intervals. However, this does not give us the ability to react immediately to changes in use that might threaten the health of the system.

Solution

Leveraging enterprise monitoring and management to report the status of all system elements at an appropriate frequency. Implement an automated monitoring and alerting process that watches for indicators of a failing system and warns the system operations team--allowing them to take preventative action if possible. The architecture includes a monitoring component that *watches* a defined set of resources for each of the system elements. Predefined thresholds are established for the different types of resource--if any system element reaches one of these thresholds an alert is sent to the operations team warning them of the possibility of failure.

This pattern applies to all system elements that generate status information, regardless of whether they are hardware or software.

Impact on NFRs

This describes the impact on NFRs of the enterprise monitoring solution pattern:

NFRs	Description
Availability	The alerts can help the operations team prevent the system from becoming partially or wholly unavailable.
Performance	Performance is negatively impacted because a reasonably high level of continuous reporting is required on some system elements to support the necessary level of monitoring.
Scalability	Not affected.
Security	Not affected.
Manageability	Manageability is improved as there is no need to monitor the system manually.
Maintainability	Not affected.
Flexibility	Not affected.
Portability	Not affected.
Cost	Cost is increased, regardless of whether a specific management application is purchased or custom solutions are built. This cost is justified as it makes the system manageable for less money than employing many operations people.

Demilitarized zone

Applications, particularly those facing the public Internet, are regularly subject to attacks on their functionality, resources, and information.

Context

The application holds information on users and provides valuable functionality for users. The application is exposed to an environment which contains potential attackers. The system holds customer information, order information and commercially sensitive sales information, any of which could be stolen or corrupted by an attacker. This information will be shared across corporate systems making them liable to attack as well.

Drivers

Drivers for the demilitarized zone solution pattern include:

- The risk of attack will be higher if the potential rewards from the attack are high in terms of financial gain or publicity. Any countermeasure must be commensurate with the perceived threat.
- We must make intrusion into both the hosting company's systems and the web application itself as difficult as possible.
- We want to make the system open and easy to use for legitimate users, but as the level of security is increased it becomes harder to use the system.

Solution

Provide a region of the system that is separate from both the external users and the internal data and functionality--commonly known as a **Demilitarized Zone** (**DMZ**). Restrict access to this region from the outside by means of limiting network traffic flow to certain physical servers. Use the same techniques to limit access from servers in the DMZ to the internal systems.

Architecture implements a DMZ by deploying its dedicated web and application servers on opposite sides of a firewall. The internal firewall will only allow through traffic from the web servers to dedicated locations and ports on the application servers. All other access to internal resources is denied. The web servers and the internal firewall are also defended by a filtering router connected to the outside world.

This pattern usually requires a combination of hardware and software.

Impact on NFRs

This describes the impact of the NRFs of the DMZ solution pattern.

NFRs	Description
Availability	Availability may be negatively impacted as the firewall becomes a single point of failure (standard procedure is for a firewall to 'fail closed', that is, in the event of a failure it will deny all connections to the protected systems).
Performance	There is a potential negative impact on performance due to the overhead of network traffic filtering and the necessity for physical separation between the web servers and the application servers as defined in dedicated Web and application servers (although splitting the servers may actually improve performance).
Scalability	The scalability of the underlying application is not affected. However, additional elements (such as filtering routers and firewall software) must be able to scale to the desired number of users and concurrent connections.
Security	Security is improved because fewer systems are exposed to attack and multiple firewall artifacts must be breached to compromise security.
Manageability	Manageability is negatively impacted by the very restrictions that limit access to internal data and may make it difficult to access the application from an internal monitor.
Maintainability	Not affected.
Flexibility	Not affected.
Portability	Not affected.
Cost	Cost is increased as extra elements must be procured to build the DMZ. These include not only the filtering routers, firewall software, and firewall host but also the additional network equipment, such as switches and cabling, used in the DMZ itself.

Summary

This chapter outlined the patterns for NFRs, providing insights into architectural patterns and their impact on NFRs. The chapter covered all the key tiers/layers that are critical for any project and described various patterns pertaining to the business, database and integration tiers. It also covered the impact of the patterns on various NFRs. This chapter also described the trade-offs between various NFRs and the best practices to be applied on engagements.

This next chapter deals with the measurement of NFRs. It outlines four methodologies for NFR monitoring and measurement. This includes sizing, analytical modelling, quality assurance, and monitoring and management. It also describes, in depth, the approach for monitoring and measuring NFRs.

6
Sizing, Measurement and Monitoring

Software quality is commonly described in terms of what are known as non-functional requirements. An NFR is a quality of a software system that will be adjudged directly by stakeholders. Quality attributes are quantifiable by appropriate and practical scales of measure. To be effective, NFRs need to be, not only defined, but also approved and enforced. The following diagram depicts the four different approaches to NFR measurement.

The key topics covered in this chapter related to NFRs are:

- Measuring and monitoring
- Sizing
- Analytical modeling
- Quality Assurance

NFR - Sizing

Software Non-functional Assessment Process (SNAP), a measurement of non-functional software size. SNAP point sizing is a complement to a function point sizing, which measures functional software size. It is a product of the **International Function Point Users Group (IFPUG)**, and is sized using the SNAP manual.

The overall size of software consists of separate components, functional and non-functional, for example, 400 function points and 200 SNAP points. The two sizes do not sum up to one single size. The IFPUG functional sizing methodology does not change when measuring the non-functional requirements using SNAP. Non-functional sizing requires recognition of similar artifacts of software used to measure functional size, for example, **data element types (DETs)** and **file types referenced (FTRs)**.

Separating functional and non-functional requirements is important when performing a cost forecast (or other forecast, such as scheduling or staffing) for software development. In principle, a cost forecast can now be made for the function point development effort, and a second forecast must be made for the SNAP development effort. The sum of both efforts will support the best estimate of the total effort for the software development.

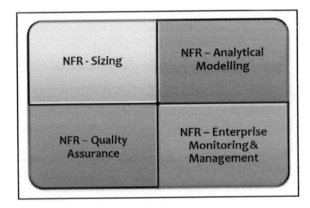

Figure 1: NFR measurement approaches

NFR - Analytical modeling

Analytical models are the products of the engineering sciences. A performance model in this category is a set of lower-level system parameters and a mathematical rule of combination that predicts the performance parameter of interest from lower-level values.

The model is normally accompanied by a performance budget or a set of nominal values for the lower-level parameters to meet a required performance target.

Please refer to the following figure for more clarity:

NFRs Measurement Techniques				
	Sizing Methodology	Analytical Modelling	Simulation	Monitoring & Management
Flexibility	HIGH	MEDIUM	MEDIUM	HIGH
Scalability	HIGH	MEDIUM	HIGH	HIGH
Accuracy	HIGH	LOW	MEDIUM	HIGH
Maturity	HIGH	MEDIUM	HIGH	HIGH
Cost	HIGH	HIGH	MEDIUM	LOW
Effectiveness	HIGH	MEDIUM	HIGH	MEDIUM
KPI Management	LOW	LOW	HIGH	MEDIUM
Strategy	HIGH	MEDIUM	HIGH	HIGH

(Alignment)

Figure 2: Comparison NFR measurement techniques

NFR - Simulation

Non-functional simulation (testing) targets non-functional requirements: the way a system performs, rather than specific behaviors. This is in contrast to functional testing, which targets functional requirements that describe the functions of a system and components. The names of non-functional tests are often used interchangeably because of the overlap between various non-functional requirements.

For example, performance is a broad term and will have coverage for attributes like reliability and scalability.

Non-functional testing is concerned with NFRs and is designed specifically to evaluate the readiness of a system according to the various quality attributes which are not covered by frequent functional testing. For example, in functional testing, it might be revealed that the function of inputting data into a set of cells within a database works, but usability testing (a part of non-functional testing) shows that persisting a version of the document requires two minutes, which will be reviewed as too long a time frame.

Non-functional testing allows us to measure and compare the results of testing the non-functional qualities of systems, for example, by testing the application against a performance requirement. Basically, non-functional testing demonstrates how well the product performances as opposed to simply how the product behaves.

NFRs tend to be those that reflect the quality attributes of the software, particularly in the context of the suitability perspective of its end users. It can begin after the completion of functional testing. The non-functional tests are made effective by using testing tools. Non-functional testing has a significant influence on customer and user satisfaction.

Types of non-functional requirements are represented as follows:

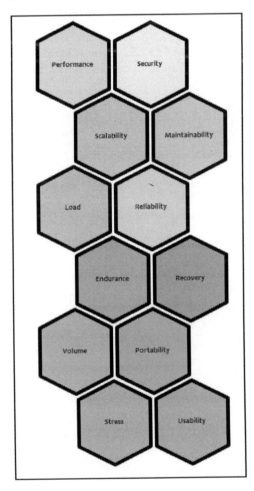

Figure 3: NFR testing

Types of non-functional testing

The types of non-functional testing are as follows:

Performance Testing

Conducted to determine how fast the system performs under a specific load. This serves various purposes, such as demonstrating that the system meets performance requirements. One can compare two systems to find out which performs better. Alternatively, it can measure what part of the system or workload causes system bottlenecks:

- Validates that the application meets the expected response time
- Conducted as a part of integration testing
- Conducted as a part of systems testing

Scalability testing

Conducted for measuring the systems capability to scale up in terms of capabilities like workload supported, the number of transactions, data volume, and so on.

Load testing

Conducted to understand the behavior of the system under a specific user load. This is carried out to determine a system's behavior under both normal and peak loads. This helps to understand the maximum capacity of an application as well as any bottlenecks and element causing this degradation:

- Validates that the application performs as expected when concurrent users access the application, and registers expected response time
- Conducted with multiple user loads to get response time and throughput of the application

Endurance testing

Involves testing a system with a significant user load extended over a long time span, to discover how the system behaves under sustained user load. For example, an application may behave exactly as expected when tested for one hour, but when the same application is tested for three hours, problems such as memory leaks cause the system to act randomly or fail.

Volume testing

Testing an application with a certain amount of data, for example, testing the application with a specific database size, expand the database size and then test the application's performance on it.

- Subjecting the application to significant amounts of data and checking the threshold where the application fails
- Maximum database size is created, and multiple users query the database or create a large report

Stress testing

Involves testing beyond normal operational capacity, often to its breaking point, in order to detect the outcome. This form of testing is used to determine the stability of an application. This test puts emphasis on robustness, availability, and exception handling under a large load. The goals are to ensure the application does not crash in conditions of insufficient resources, such as memory, CPU, or disk space.

- Done on low memory or low disk space to reveals the defects that cannot be found under normal conditions
- Multiple users load the same transactions on the same data
- Multiple user loads connected to servers with different workloads
- Reduce think time to zero to stress the servers to their limit

Security testing

Checks whether the application is secured. It is a process to determine that an application protects data and maintains integrity as intended. To ensure that no one can hack the system or log in the application without proper authorization.

Maintainability testing

It's done to find how easy it is to maintain the system. Relates to how easy it is to analyze, change and test the application.

Reliability testing

The objective of reliability testing is to determine the reliability of the system and to determine whether the software is capable of recovering from an unexpected error or exception condition gracefully.

Recovery testing

It's done in order to check how fast the application can recover after it has gone through a crash or hardware failure etc. Recovery testing is the forced failure of the system in a variety of ways to verify that recovery is properly made:

- Power interruption, while doing CURD operations
- Invalid keys and database pointers
- Database process is prematurely terminated or aborted
- Database fields, keys, and pointers are corrupted manually
- Physically disconnect the communication wires, turn off power, turn down the routers and network servers

Usability testing

Usability testing tests the ease with which the user interfaces can be leveraged. It tests whether the application is user-friendly or not. Usability testing includes the following five components:

- **Memorability**: When users return to the system after an extended period of time, do the users remember enough to use it effectively next time, or do they have to start learning all over again?
- **Efficiency**: How fast can experienced users accomplish certain tasks?
- **Satisfaction**: How much does the user enjoy using the system?
- **Errors**: How many errors do end-users make, how severe are these errors and how easily can end users recover from these errors?
- **Learnability**: How easy is it for end users to accomplish basic tasks the first time they are leveraging the UI?

Enterprise Monitoring and Management - EMM

Application Performance Management (APM) / Enterprise Monitoring and Management (EMM) is the name given to the use of technology to initiate, deploy, monitor, fix, update and optimize systems within an organization. Application management software employs measurements of response times and other component and resource interactions, to help manage the overall stability and usability of the software within its purview.

APM tools are illustrated as follows:

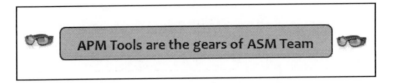

Figure 4: APM tools

APM is a $2 billion market for application performance monitoring, as predicted by Gartner. Business and C-level executives recognize that IT is not just infrastructure that supports background workflows, but is a direct generator of revenues and a key enabler of strategy.

APM functional blocks are illustrated as follows:

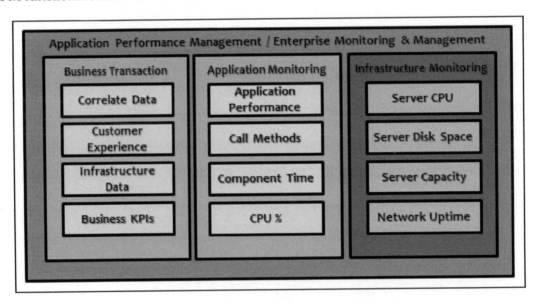

Figure 5: APM Layers

Challenges faced by the ASM teams:

Applications have become difficult to monitor, architectures have become more modular, redundant, distributed, dynamic, and boundaries are blurring; often the code execution path taking multiple routes during execution.

The combined impact of modularity, redundancy, distribution and dynamism may subside the effectiveness of the techniques that traditionally drive the APM landscape.

The following diagram lists the typical challenges faced by ASM teams:

Challenge	Description
Application architecture	Application architectures have become increasingly modular and distributed. Application architectures have evolved in to make monitoring application performance a real challenge.
Application maintainability	Data centers supports users and customers across the globe. The ability to maintain application identity across time has become increasingly challenging. The trend has been toward breaking down application business logic into more self-contained components, for agility to address the changing business demands.
Development methodology	Application development methodologies such as Agile, accelerate the rate at which changes are injected into application code running in production.
Application boundaries	The boundaries between one application and another have become blurred and it's almost impossible to attribute any specific quantity of resource consumption to one set of application users or another.
Technology complexity	The implications of late-binding technologies are such that, what appears to the user as repeated executions of the same transaction from one day to the next, are in fact realized by very different paths across the infrastructure and may result in very different levels of resource consumption.
APM tools	Inability of application monitoring tools to look deep into the situation. Script creation and maintenance is an intensive and ongoing process. Vendor-driven and fragmented toolsets.

Management challenges	Focus on changing the statistics rather than improving the customer experience Product focus to extent that process and people are neglected. Dealing with multiple/difficult vendors for the application stack and problem resolution. Maintaining or reducing the TCO. Ability of the APM suites to find, isolate and diagnose problems anywhere in the application stack.

Monitoring landscape

APM is not merely an end-user monitoring application. APM is part of the IT infrastructure and the use of the tools that is divided over many stakeholders. The following diagram is an APM reference architecture that incorporates best practices, standards and learning from the past engagements.

These are the different areas of the landscape that are monitored through a combination of various tools. Finally, the significant bit is correlating the information from different sources within the application landscape and is required for the single glass pane view for an enterprise which is also part of the ASM tools monitoring scope:

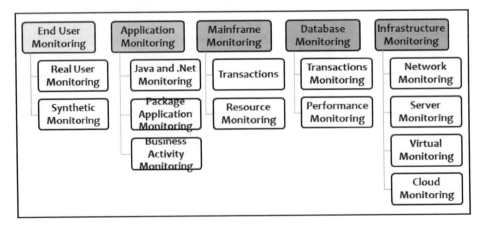

Figure 6: APM monitoring landscape

Functionality - dimensions

APM tools leverage these dimensions to generate meaningful data for the IT support and operations teams. APM techniques are sub-divided into five dimensions of functionality:

- Discovery, modeling, and display
- End user experience monitoring
- Component deep-dive monitoring
- User-defined transaction profiling
- Application performance analytics

The following diagram is:

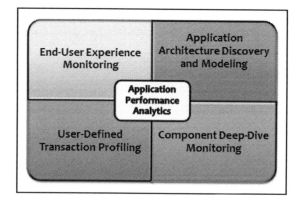

Figure 7: APM dimensions

End-user experience monitoring

There are two different types of end user monitoring techniques:

Real user monitoring:

This technique requires the placement of software bots at various locations within the data center predominantly around the dynamic elements like switches, bridges, routers, gateways. This is also known as the **first mile monitoring**.

Synthetic

The oldest approach to capturing end-user experience data involving running scripts against an application in production and record response time and availability results. This is also known as **last mile monitoring**.

Discovery, modeling, and display

These technologies discover what software and hardware components are exercised as user-defined transactions are executed, and how those components are related to one another.

- **Transaction profile**: Models built from reports generated in from the user defined transaction dimension of APM
- **Service dependency mapping**: Technologies for discovering how different types of traffic flow among various types of physical and virtual infrastructure elements
- **Bayesian networks**: Intended to display random variables describing statistical properties of a system's behavior, while the links among the variables represent the conditional observational dependence of one variable on another.
- **Network topologies**: Intended primarily to display physical devices and the physical links that allow these devices to communicate with one another.

User defined transactions

Historically, this meant a logical unit of work. In the context of APM, however, the term *transaction* means something different. In a composite application, users or customers will typically perform a number of distinct operations that, however un-connected they may be from the point of view of the systems being accessed and exercised, form an integral action from the perspective of that user or customer. This *integral action* is what most APM vendors mean by the term *transaction*. The user-defined transaction profiling technologies will attempt to trace the effects of this transaction across an array of components and network paths.

Component deep dive monitoring

The fourth dimension refers to a broad collection of technologies and products designed to monitor the performance of the various hardware and software components that support the execution of an application.

What distinguishes component deep-dive monitoring in application context from performance monitoring technology, in general, is the ability to associate the latency or resource consumption being measured with the application causing the latency or resource consumption. In practice, such monitoring is widely confined to off-the-shelf application stacks, middle ware (for example, application servers, message queuing systems, and service buses), **database management systems (DBMS)** and aspects of network packet flow.

Application performance analytics

Analytics are brought to bear to establish the root cause in the middle of the vast volumes of data generated in the first four steps, as well as to anticipate better and prepare for end user experience problems that could emerge in the future.

Monitoring tools - managing the problem

APM monitoring model: the following section list of steps required for managing the problem in the application landscape.

- Collect response times by transaction and determine the first level alerting criterion. This is best achieved by using:
    - Passive agent that provides true end user performance.
    - Active agent that provides availability data.
- Understand and map all the components of the transaction. Several solutions are possible, but we believe that this model must be able to track each type of transaction, or each transaction, through the infrastructure, provide a template for debugging performance problems, and give full visibility into the transaction path. In addition, this dependency data should be available to improve the mapping of dependencies in a CMDB or CMS.
- Monitor applications built leveraging the Java EE and .Net frameworks.
- A connector is leveraged to collect performance data coming from mainframe-based transactions using IBM CICS/DB2 or IMS, messaging technologies such as WebSphere MQ or MQSeries between distributed systems and mainframes.
- Monitor packaged applications provided by vendors such as SAP, Oracle, or other ISVs, and custom applications not written in Java.
- Monitor the physical and virtual components of the infrastructure.
- Monitor performance of the database(s). This includes the ability to analyze specific database performance issues.
- Provide all this information on a *single-pane-of-glass* dashboard.

- Combine all these parameters, which leads to the ability to determine an alert, identify the root cause of this alert, and if possible predict an impending performance issue.

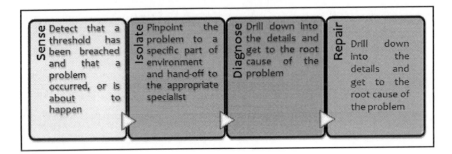

Figure 8: APM problem resolution

APM dashboard

The following sections deep dive into the various aspects of dashboards for different APM domains along with the explanation placed as follows:

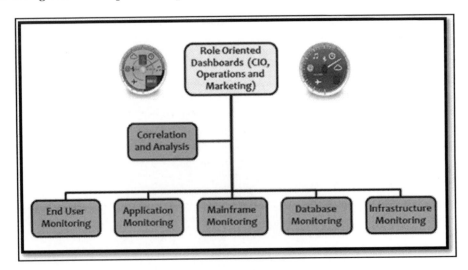

Figure 9: APM dashboards

- **Real User Monitoring**: Performance from your actual users, visitor paths, impact of geography, ISP, browser size and type, operating system, device and cache, performance degradation, and availability data

- **Synthetic Monitoring**: Performance based on the scripts, browser size and type, operating system, device and cache, performance degradation, ND availability data
- **Business Activity Monitoring**: Customer journeys (average journey fulfillment) and holdings
- **Application Monitoring**: Response times, transactions per second, user logged in per second
- **Mainframes**: Transaction mapping processor complex, LPAR and operating system, address Spaces/jobs, STC's, IDMS subsystems, datacom subsystems, DB2 subsystems, CICS regions, IMS subsystems, MQ subsystems, tape, and DASD
- **Database Monitoring**: Transaction rates, database query response times, disk u, CPU utilization, and number of active users
- **Network**: Network throughput, current logon, failover monitoring, other network monitoring points
- **Infrastructure Servers Monitoring**: Hard disk utilization, files open/Owner, file existence monitor, file size, memory utilization, CPU utilization, processes
- **Role-Based Dashboards**: Performance and availability indicators for critical applications, locations and supporting infrastructure across the enterprise, performance problems for the busiest URLs, supplemented with usage, performance and availability metrics, including the number of users

APM future roadmap

One of the approaches is to analyze the current APM maturity and then recommend a technology adoption road map based on the business goals and objective considering the complexity.

There is additional emphasis on end user monitoring, so the support team must ensure that end user experience always meets expectations. The rule of thumb is that if there is a problem, find out before the customer complains. The APM landscape consists of a combination of agent and agentless monitoring starting with agentless for fast initial deployment.

One of the major concerns in APM landscape is the virtualized infrastructure which impacts the metrics that are gathered from the guest OS, and this requires a new approach to APM tuned to the needs of virtualized systems.

Summary

This chapter dealt with the measurement of NFRs. It outlined four methodologies for NFRs monitoring and measurement. These include sizing, analytical modeling, quality assurance and monitoring and management. This chapter also described the approach in depth for monitoring and measuring NFRs.

The next, and final, chapter of the book provides a summary and trends for the NFR domain. It also outlines architecture assessment and NFR measurement methodology.

7

Understanding Pivotal NFRs and Closing Thoughts

This appendix includes checklists for the software quality attributes that are not covered in earlier chapters. For each attribute, the checklist includes the business, application, data, and infrastructure domains. The measures with a positive influence are indicated with a + plus sign, those with a negative influence are preceded by a - minus sign. There is always the possibility of investigating a specific quality characteristic in a given organization using a standard checklist. Therefore, the checklists in this chapter serve as references for organization independent checklists that may even be project independent.

Pivotal NFRs

The following diagram depicts the different pivotal NFRs that are covered in this chapter:

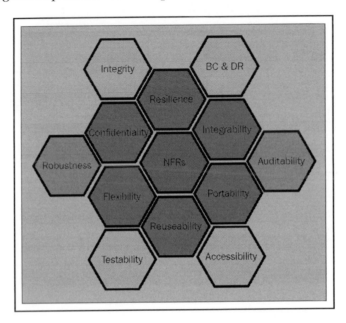

Pivotal NFRs KPI and framework

The following table and diagram depict the pivotal NFRs KPIs and frameworks:

NFR	Attributes
Integrity	Mean time to integrate with a new interfacing system Ability of a system to perform its required functions under stated conditions for a specific period of time Data integrity: Referential integrity in database tables and interfaces Application integrity and information integrity--during transactions Fault trapping (I/O): Handling failures and recovery
Business continuity	RTO/Restore time: Time required switching to secondary site when the primary fails RPO/Backup time: Time taken to back your data

Resilience	Length of time between failures Recoverability: Time required by the system to resume operations in the event of failure Resilience: The reliability characteristics of the system and sub-components
Confidentiality	Encryption (data in flight and at rest): All external communications between the system's data server and clients must be encrypted Data confidentiality: All data must be protectively marked, stored and protected Compliance: The process to confirm systems compliance with the organizations security standards and policies
Integratability	Mean time to integrate with a new interfacing system Compatibility with shared applications: Other systems it need to integrate Compatibility with third-party applications: Other systems that it has to live with amicably
Robustness	Percentage of failures due to invalid data/input Degree of service degradation Minimum performance under extreme user loads Active services in presence of faults Length of time for which the system is required to manage stress conditions
Auditability	System must maintain full traceability of transactions Audited objects and audited database fields to be included for auditing File characteristics: Size before, size after, structure User and transactional time stamps Get notices and alerts as thresholds (for example, storage, memory, processor) are approached Remotely manage systems and create new virtual instances at the click of a button Rich graphical dashboard for all key application metrics System must maintain full traceability of transactions Audited objects and audited database fields to be included for auditing User and transactional time stamps, and so on

Flexibility	Conformance to design standards, coding standards, best practices, reference architectures and frameworks. Flexibility: The degree to which the system is intended to support change Release support: The way in which the system will support the introduction of initial release, phased rollouts and future releases Handle new information types Manage new or changed business entities Consume or provide new feeds
Portability	Number of targeted platforms (hardware, OS) Proportion of platform specific components or functionality Mean time to port to a different platform
Reusability	Percentage of reused requirements, design elements, code, tests, and so on Coupling of components Degree of use of frameworks
Testability	Time to run tests Time to setup development and execution testing environment Probability of visible failure in presence of a defect Test coverage (requirements coverage, code coverage)
Accessibility	Look and feel standards: Screen element density, layout and flow, colors, UI metaphors, keyboard shortcuts Internationalization/Localization requirements: Languages, spellings, keyboards, paper sizes, and so on.

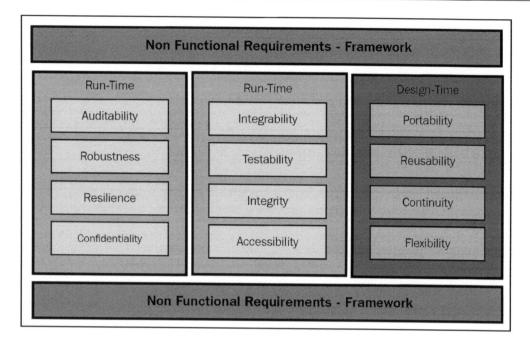

Pivotal NFR classification

This section describes pivotal NFRs and its various domain checklists.

Integrity

The degree to which the information is accurate and authentic.

Infrastructure domain

Will a different identification (user-ID) and authentication (password) be used for the test environment and the production environment?

Business domain

The following is the domain checklist:

- Has the security within the user organization been arranged (see checklist for security)?
- Is an efficient production scheme set up with a balanced regulation of priorities between the applications and with the supporting functions, such as the back-up procedure?
- Is access to the computer center restricted to the people who belong there?
- Is the computer center housed in a building that is optimally proof against stroke of lightning, fire, electricity failure, and water damage?
- Will the input be checked?
- Are passwords being used?
- Will attempts for access be checked?
- Has the choice for subsystems been argued?
- Have all integrity needs been addressed?
- Is the solution capable of functioning correctly--or at the very minimum not failing catastrophically--under many conditions?
- Describe tools or instrumentation that are available that monitor the health and performance of the system.
- Describe what form of audit logs are in place to capture system history, particularly after a mishap.
- Describe the capabilities of the system to dispatch its own error messages to service personnel.

Application domain

The following is the domain checklist:

- Has use been made of applied national or international standards, for instance to exchange of data via networks (OSI, TCP/IP, XML), of applications in the IBM-environment (SAA), or of a standard programming language that can be compiled on a wide variety of hardware?
- Is a specific application present and in use for security?
- Are input, output, and processing implemented separately?
- Has data consistency been taken care of by use of checkpoint/restart utilities?
- Will the data processing be done dually?

- Has the data processing been split up into sub-transactions?
- Is the operator able to supply status information?
- Have check processes (watchdogs) been applied?
- Are the subsystems distributed?
- Are the program modules being reused?
- Is use made of technical actions in interfaces?
- Are the algorithms optimized, that is, for performance reasons?
- Will user input be completed automatically?
- Have you planned how your software architecture will be validated throughout its development?
- Have you identified suitable validation techniques for use at each stage of the life cycle? Do you know when you will use each?

Data domain

The following is the domain checklist:

- Do you have clear strategies for transactional consistency across distributed data stores, and do these balance this need with the cost in terms of performance and complexity?
- Do you have mechanisms in place for validating migrated data and dealing appropriately with errors?
- Have you defined sufficient storage and processing capacity for archiving, and for restoring archived data?
- Has a data quality assessment been done? Have you created strategies for dealing with poor quality data?
- Is there a clear system-level concurrency model?
- Are your models at the right level of abstraction? Have you focused on the architecturally significant aspects?
- Can you simplify your concurrency design?
- Do all interested parties understand the overall concurrency strategy?
- Have you mapped all functional elements to a process (and thread if necessary)?
- Do you have a state model for at least one functional element in each process and thread? If not, are you sure the processes and threads will interact safely?
- Have you defined a suitable set of inter-process communication mechanisms to support the inter-element interactions defined in the functional view?
- Are all shared resources protected from corruption?

- Have you minimized the inter-task communication and synchronization required?
- Do you have any resource hot spots in your system? If so, have you estimated the likely throughput, and is it high enough? Do you know how you would reduce contention at these points if forced to later?
- Can the system possibly deadlock? If so, do you have a strategy for recognizing and dealing with this when it occurs?
- Will a periodic check be done on the consistency of the database and datasets?
- Is the data storage distributed?
- What are the data model, data definitions, structure, and hosting options of purchased applications (COTS)?
- What are the rules for defining and maintaining the data requirements and designs for all components of the information system?
- What shareable repository is used to capture the model content and the supporting information for data?
- What is the physical data model definition (derived from logical data models) used to design the database?
- What software development and data management tools have been selected?
- Which data owners have been identified to be responsible for common data definitions, eliminating unplanned redundancy, providing consistently reliable, timely, and accurate information, and protecting data from misuse and destruction?
- Is the data encrypted?
- Is data quality covered in the scope?
- Does architecture allow for implementation of all the key requirements?
    - Data migration
    - Data quality
    - Data validations, verifications and mapping rules
    - Data synchronization
- Are the data quality requirements from the business user needs been addresses?
- Does the data architecture communicate an adequate vision of the system that will direct further design activities?
- Are the KPIs and KRAs for data domain adequately addressed?
- Are all interfaces between the source and target systems identified and justified?
- Has the data referential integrity and/or normalization been described?
- Are data synchronization needs addressed? Does it cater to both real-time and batch modes?

- Will the proposed data architecture satisfy all specified quality attributes and performance goals?
- Are the data model, data definitions, structure, and hosting options considered?
- Is the data quality strategy described and justified?
- Have all the data models that are part of the scope been addressed and described?
    - B2B
    - B2C
- Are the data access requirements for standard file, message, data management, and decision support systems described?
- Have all the physical and logical data models been described?
- Are design decisions and assumptions documented explicitly and motivated?
- Are the mapping rules adequately captured and documented for the data domain?
- Have the data storage and retention considerations been addressed?
- Have the quality assurance considerations been addressed?
- Have all backup and recovery needs been addressed?
- Have migration/conversion considerations been addressed?

Infrastructure domain

The following is the domain checklist:

- Is a modern programming environment used, which enforces consistency in reference to data and functions?
- Have hardware, network, PCs, system software and DBMS been chosen which are geared to one another and to the applications?
- Have hardware suppliers been chosen who will offer adequate support during the life cycle of the information system?
- Has the definition been made objectively of the requisite processing and data storage capacity for the information system (centrally and de-centrally) to comply with all functional and quality requirements?
- Will a diagnosis of the hardware, the network, and so on, be made periodically?
- Is a dual set of hardware, and so on, available for alternative use?

Business continuity

The ability to recover from and continue service following a major incident such as the loss of an entire data center.

Business domain

The following is the domain checklist:

- Has the choice for subsystems been argued?
- Are well-trained substitutes on standby within the production organization?
- Are well-trained substitutes on standby within the user organization?
- Is there insurance against the risk of damage caused by faults or disruptions in the information services?
- Are the backups of vital data stored in a special, extra security location, preferably outside the computer center?
- Have provisions been made so that, in the instance of serious disturbances or disasters, information services may continue as seamlessly as possible?
- Has a similar production environment been reserved, for instance in a different computer center, including accompanying procedures for alternative use?
- Have manual procedures been prepared in order to substitute (parts of) the automated information services?
- Has it been determined whether additional education is required to operate the new or changed information system?
- Does an adequate procedure exist in the instance of a disturbance?
- Is the hardware, and so on, insured?
- Is a plan for disasters available?
- Is the access to the organization grounds and buildings controlled?
- Have measures been taken to prevent, signal, or take care of technical disturbances and disasters?
- Are the backups of vital data stored in a special, extra security location, preferably outside the computer center?
- Is access to the computer center restricted to the people who belong there?
- Do you have a description of the instrumentation included in the application that allows for the health and performance of the application to be monitored?
- What is the frequency of software changes that must be distributed?

- What tools are used for software distribution?
- Are multiple software and/or data versions allowed in production?
- What is the user data backup frequency and expected restore time?
- How are user accounts created and managed?
- What is the system license management strategy?
- What general system administration tools are required?
- What specific application administration tools are required?
- What specific service administration tools are required?
- How are service calls received and dispatched?

Application domain

The following is the domain checklist:

- Has use been made of applied international standards, for instance to exchange of data via networks (OSI, TCP/IP, XML), of applications in the IBM-environment (SAA) or of a standard programming language, which can be compiled on a wide variety of hardware?
- Does a back-up and recovery system containing procedures and executables exist for:
    - Periodic saving of a coherent set copies of datasets
    - Logging of all transactions starting from the last generation
    - Reprocessing of all logged transactions
- Will the recovery procedure be tested periodically?
- Have check processes (watchdogs) been applied?
- Has the consistency of data been taken care of by use of checkpoint/restart utilities?
- Are the subsystems distributed?
- Is the essential functionality stored in separate modules?
- Will the data processing be done dually?
- Are automatic alternative facilities built in?
- Does an actual overview of all used programs, including version numbers, exist?
- The recoverability is influenced considerably by the maintainability regarding the technical system architecture (see checklist for maintainability)
- Have the functions been modelled in coherence with the company business process model?
- Has the choice for subsystems been argued?

- Is the data processing functionally structured in such a way that it is possible to continue the processing of data when some non-essential parts of the information system are shut down?
- Can availability requirements be met by the chosen hardware and software platform?
- Have you defined strategies for disaster recovery and business continuity?
- Do stakeholders have realistic expectations around unplanned downtime?
- Checklist for architecture definition
- Does the proposed architectural solution meet the availability requirements?
- Can this be demonstrated, either theoretically, or based on previous practical experience?
- Does the solution consider the time taken to recover from failure, for example, to restore from backup if necessary?
- Does the backup solution provide for the transactional integrity of restored data?
- Does the backup solution support online backup, with acceptable degradation in performance? If not, is it feasible to take the system down in order to perform backups?
- Has consideration been given to restoring data from corrupt or incomplete backups?
- Will the system respond gracefully to software errors, logging, and reporting them appropriately?
- Have you defined a standby site in the architecture, if appropriate? Is the standby site configured identically to the production site, or will it offer reduced performance? If the latter, is this reduced performance acceptable to the users?
- Have you defined and tested mechanisms for switching from production to standby environments? If not, when will you do this?
- Have you assessed the impact of the availability solution on functionality and performance? Is this impact acceptable?
- If high availability is particularly important, have you assessed the architecture for single points of failure and other weaknesses?
- If you've developed a fault-tolerant model, does this extend to all vulnerable components (such as disk controllers)?

Data domain

The following is the domain checklist:

- Is the data storage distributed?
- Are utilities available for analysis and reorganization of the database?
- Does an overview of all used datasets exist?
- Do you know how information will be moved from the existing environment into the new system?
- Do you have a clear migration strategy to move workload to the new system?
- Can you reverse the migration if you need to? How will you deal with data synchronization (if required)?
- Do you know how the system will be backed up? Are you confident that the approach identified will allow reliable system restoration in an acceptable time period?
- Are the administrators confident that they can monitor and control the system in production?
- Do the administrators have a clear understanding of the procedures they need to perform for the system?
- How will performance metrics be captured for the system's elements?
- Can you manage the configuration of all the system's elements?
- Do you know how support will be provided for the system? Is the support provided suitable for the stakeholders it is being provided for?
- Have you cross-referenced the requirements of the administration model back to the development view to ensure that they will be implemented consistently?
- Is the data migration architecture compatible with the amount of time available to perform the data migration? Are there catch-up mechanisms in place where the source data is volatile during the data migration?
- Has the database access been optimized?
- Does documentation exist about the data model and is this documentation consistent?
- Is the data encrypted?
- Is the data storage distributed?

Infrastructure domain

The following is the domain checklist:

- Introduction with a summary of names, identifications, and characteristics of the functionality of the system and subsystems
- Scheme of the system structure
- Relational scheme of the run structure, with, for each run, the time, programs, indicatives per program, and estimate of time
- Contact details (name, department, telephone number)
- For each run to be executed the following data: name, identification, characteristics, system flow scheme and/or subsystem flow scheme, by which the data flows are related to parts of the configuration, and from which the interfaces with the systems or subsystems that do not belong to the run can be derived
- Does the production manual contain the following components?
- Does a production manual exist?
- Are these specific standards and norms met?
- Do specific standards and norms from the processing organization exist for resource usage, external memory, and performance?
- Is there a description of the hardware and software components for the infrastructure?
- Is a dual set of hardware, and so on, available for alternative use?
- Is a dual set of hardware, and so on, available for alternative use?
    - Receipt and preparation containing:
    - Type, source and time of receipt
    - Reception activities and checks
    - Data conversion, instructions and checks
    - Destination and actions at delivery of input media
    - Destination and the actions at delivery of basic documents
    - Preparation of production containing:
    - Time schedule
    - Description of the working procedure (jobstream)
    - Schemes for the handling of removable discs and for the storage instructions;
    - Deliverance of input
- Service manual containing:
    - General service workbook

- Service, check, and error displays together with the accompanying instructions
- Possibilities for interruption
- Instructions for restart at unplanned interruptions
- Production manual containing:
  - Handling of removable discs
  - Checks and reports
  - Completion activities
  - Delivery and distribution
  - Ultimate time of delivery
- Has the planning for production been changed, based on the new or updated information system?
- Has it been determined how to request for and plan incidental batches?
- Is an integrated test facility available?
- Is a current infrastructure in use?

Has a detailed analysis been made of the processing capacity, storage capacity, data communication hardware, and system applications?

Resilience

The reliability and resilience characteristics of the systems and its sub-components.

Business domain

The following is the domain checklist:

- Has the choice for subsystems been argued?
- Has a general reference model been used?
- Have the functions been modelled in coherence with the company business process model?
- Is open, consistent, and up-to-date functional documentation available?
- Are standards, best practices, and frameworks being used wherever possible?

- Does the architecture emphasize reusability?
- Is emphasis given to leveraging existing components in the landscape to reduce the amount of work required to build the solution?
- Are SOA principles and reference architecture defined and described?
- Are architecture principles defined and described?
- Have you defined strategies for disaster recovery and business continuity?
- Does the solution consider the time taken to recover from failure, for instance, to restore from backup if necessary?
- Does the backup solution provide for the transactional integrity of restored data?
- Does the backup solution support online backup, with acceptable degradation in performance? If not, is it feasible to take the system down in order to perform backups?
- Has consideration been given to restoring data from corrupt or incomplete backups?
- Will the system respond gracefully to software errors, logging and reporting them appropriately?
- Have you defined and tested mechanisms for switching from production to standby environments? If not, when will you do this?
- Have you assessed the impact of the availability solution on functionality and performance? Is this impact acceptable?
- If high availability is particularly important, have you assessed the architecture for single points of failure and other weaknesses?
- If you developed a fault-tolerant model, does this extend to all vulnerable components (such as disk controllers)?

Application domain

The following is the domain checklist:

- Have standards for development been used (for instance, standard scheme techniques, standards for structured programming, standards for database approach, recognizable nomenclature, and standards for the use of user interfaces)?
- Have applied national and international standards been used, for instance to exchange of data via networks (OSI, TCP/IP, XML), of applications in the IBM-environment (SAA) or of a standard programming language which can be compiled on a wide variety of hardware?

- Are the routine actions built into the interface consistent?
- Have check processes (watchdogs) been applied?
- Is the operator able to supply status information?
- Is the data processing split up into sub-transactions?
- Have the input, processing and output been implemented separately?
- Have possible machine dependencies been implemented in separate modules?
- Has the essential functionality been stored in separate modules?
- Have I/O operations been classified in separate modules in order to separate the retrieval of data from the processing of data?
- Have the programs been structured, and are they easy to understand?
- Is open, consistent, and up-to-date technical documentation available?
- Have the programs been parameterized?
- Will technical actions within the interface be used?
- Are the subsystems distributed?
- Will data processing be done dually?
- Have the algorithms been optimized?
- Are tools provided to enable customisation and development of business services? Can services be cloned? Can the tools be used by business staff to set up services?
- What proprietary technology (hardware and software) is needed for this system?
- What change control software is used to manage system version control?
- What is the change control process? Please describe this both from a business and technical perspective.
- What change control notes does the customer receive?
- What system build tools are used to create the system?
- How is the system packaged and distributed?
- How many copies of the system are needed at any one time? How is change control managed across these copies?
- Have you planned how your software architecture will be validated throughout its development?
- Have you identified suitable validation techniques for use at each stage of the lifecycle? Do you know when you will use each?
- Is it possible to restart an application after a system breakdown?
- Is it possible to restart an application after an application breakdown?

Data domain

The following is the domain checklist:

- Is the data model normalized?
- Is the data encrypted?
- Has the approach of the database been optimized?
- Are latency requirements clearly identified, and are mechanisms in place to ensure these are achieved?
- Do you have clear strategies for transactional consistency across distributed data stores, and do these balance this need with the cost in terms of performance and complexity?
- Do you have mechanisms in place for validating migrated data and dealing appropriately with errors?
- Have you defined sufficient storage and processing capacity for archiving, and for restoring archived data?
- Has a data quality assessment been done? Have you created strategies for dealing with poor-quality data?

Infrastructure domain

The following is the domain checklist:

- Is an integrated test facility available?
- Will 4GL facilities be used?
- Will an integrated functional development environment be used: Workbench (CASE-tool), text processor, and so on?
- Will an integrated technical development environment be used (modern development environment linked/integrated with a DMBS)?
- Will a code or system generator (ICASE) be used?

Confidentiality

The extent to which the data needs to be protected and kept confidential.

Business domain

The following is the domain checklist:

- Does the product documentation contain the possibilities regarding security?
- Does it explicitly state:
    - what the strategy is to security, based on aims and treatments
    - who the security employees are
    - which procedures regarding security must be followed in order to utilize the functionality optimally?
- Are jobs, authorities, and responsibilities in the organization of the information services separated clearly?
- Has a classification of documents been made, consisting of a number of classes of confidentiality?
- Has a limitation (and registration) of the circulation of classified documents to dedicated functionaries been arranged, based on this classification?
- Does a procedure exist for authorization of important documents that leave the organization?
- Does a check exist on behalf of the internal accountants on the processing of the procedures based on information produced afterwards?
- Will attention be paid to both the written and the automated fixed data?
- Will the functional separation be continued when authorizing personnel? Will authorization be given based on the need to do or need to know principle? (Does the logical access match the existing schemes for the **administrative organization (AO)**?)
- Has job separation been arranged between:
    - the one who has the authority to use functions in an information system for retrieval or updating data (end-users)
    - the one who decides who has access to specified functions (data) and to whom an account must be given about the access possibilities implemented
    - the one who is responsible for the actual authorization of the employees to functions (data)
- Will a distinction be made between the responsibilities for input, processing, correction, and checking at the granting of authorization?
- Will a distinction be made between creating, reading, updating, and deleting of data at the granting of authorization?
- Will the requirements for logical security access be taken into consideration at the distribution of data (to third parties) and at external data communication?

- Does a specific security procedure exist for functionaries who are in charge of internal control or security (that is, the system administrator)?
- Is the way the logical security access is constructed written adequately?
- Does a procedure exist with the several actions to be carried out based on the access logging or the reports made?
- Does the information system comply with legal commitments?
- Has the processing of confidential data (that is, the salary run) been classified in separate procedures, which may be processed by authorized people only?
- Is the access to the organization grounds and buildings controlled?
- Is the access to the computer centre restricted to the people who belong there?
- Information security and access considerations
- Have you identified the sensitive resources contained in the system?
- Have you identified the sets of principals who need access to the resources?
- Have you identified the system's needs for information integrity guarantees?
- Have you identified the system's availability needs?
- Have you established a security policy to define the security needs for the system, including which principals are allowed to perform which operations on which resources, and where information integrity needs to be enforced?
- Is the security policy as simple as possible?
- Have you worked through a formal threat model to identify the security risks your system faces?
- Have you worked through example scenarios with your stakeholders so that they understand the planned security policy and the security risks the system runs?
- Have you reviewed your security requirements with external experts?
- Do guidelines exist for the restriction of the access to the applications?
- Are passwords being used?
- Will access attempts be checked?

Application domain

The following is the domain checklist:

- Are the possibilities that exist to restrict access to the system software, documents, and datasets utilized as best as possible?
- Is there, within the security access, functionality for identification, authentication, authorization, logging, and reporting distinguished?

- Is it possible to make a difference between the responsibilities for input, processing, correction, and checking of the granting of authorization?
- Is it possible to make a difference between input, change, query, and removal of data at the granting of authorization?
- Has consideration been made for the requirements of the (logical) security access with external data communication?
- Will the users maintain their own passwords and are they responsible for the use of their user-IDs and passwords?
- Does a (technical) procedure exist for the changing of passwords periodically?
- Does the system enforce the use of 'strong' passwords (minimum length, not only lower case letters, but also upper case, numbers or special characters)?
- Is there a restriction on the number of possible attempts to log in?
- Is the input and storage of passwords conducted in such a way that third parties cannot recognize them?
- Will the security access be violated by the use of query languages?
- Will any unsuccessful attempts for use be logged?
- Have measures been taken for the restriction of the period for free access to the terminal (that is, automatic log-off)?
- Is a specific application present and in use for security?
- Will the memory be cleared after processing?
- Are the subsystems distributed?
- Will the data processing be done dually?
- Does the infrastructure architecture cover backups, storage databases, servers, hardware, licensing areas?
- Does it address various considerations around the SDLC environment; for example, development, staging, pre-production, and production?
- Is the security architecture defined and described?
- Are different security architecture cover identification and authorization, SSO, audit trail, and logging?
- Is the authentication, authorization and identification mechanism described as applicable to various applications, systems and users?
- Does the Security Architecture cover users, systems, and network aspects?
- Have you addressed each threat identified in the threat model to the extent required?
- Have you used as much third-party security technology as possible?
- Have you produced an integrated overall design for the security solution?

- Have you considered all standard security principles when designing your security infrastructure?
- Is your security infrastructure as simple as possible?
- Have you defined how security breaches will be identified and how to recover from breaches?
- Have you applied the results of the security perspective to all of the affected views?
- Have external experts reviewed your security design?
- Will backups be made automatically?
- Have check processes (watchdogs) been applied?
- Is the input, the output and the processing implemented separately?
- Is the operator able to supply status information?
- Has the consistency of data been taken care for by use of the checkpoint/restart utilities?
- Have national, international, or company standards been used, for instance to exchange of data via networks (OSI, TCP/IP, XML), of applications in the IBM-environment (SAA) or of a standard programming language?
- Has a standard machine interface been used?
- Are the routine actions built into the interface consistent?
- Is there a description of the user applications and standard modules (including version numbers) required at installation?
- Have standards for nomenclature been used?
- Is it possible to perform each function (including the non-logical) at least once?
- Are the subsystems distributed?
- Are the programs parameterized?

Data domain

The following is the domain checklist:

- Is the data encrypted?
- Will the data that is sent over the network be encrypted?
- Is the data storage distributed?
- Does a backup and recovery system containing procedures and executables exist for:

- Periodic saving of a coherent set of copies of datasets
- Logging of all transactions starting from the last generation
- Reprocessing of all logged transactions

- Does the back-up procedure determine when the datasets and database need to be secured and how long these back-ups should be kept?
- Is a description of the required authorizations available?
- Is a procedure for the maintenance of the authorizations available?
- Is a specific application present and in use for security (that is, RACF)?
- Do specific standards and normsexist for input, batch processing, online processing, output, and security?
- Are these specific standards and norms met?
- Are all transactions registered, that is, logged?
- Will the data processing be done dually?

Integratability

The ease with which an interconnection with a different information system or within the information system can be made and modified. Measures ability to make separated components work together

Business domain

The following is the domain checklist:

- Will a different identification (user-ID) and authentication (password) be used for the test environment and the production environment?
- Has use been made of a general reference model?
- Has the choice for subsystems been argued?
- Does the documentation state which measurements are available to prevent faulty user input and user actions?
- Does it state how recovery of faults should be done?
- Is the interaction from a user with the system written down and are his responsibilities and authorities specified?

- Is the interaction between the system and other systems specified sufficiently?
- Have sources and recipients been identified of data exchanged between the package and any existing automated or manual systems? Have separate transactions been defined for each interface to existing automated systems?
- How are user interfaces provided?
- What communication interfaces are provided, including e-mail, file exchange, and messaging?
- Describe the options for adding interfaces?
- Do the package interfaces conform to technical data standards?
- Do the package interfaces conform to any business data standards?
- Can tools be provided that can help develop and implement new interfaces?
- What are the data access requirements for standard file, message, and data management?
- What are the access requirements for decision support data?
- What are the data storage and the application logic locations?
- What query language is being used?

Application domain

The following is the domain checklist:

- Has use been made of applied national and international standards, for instance, to exchange of data via networks (OSI, TCP/IP, XML), of applications in the IBM-environment (SAA), or of a standard programming language which can be compiled on a wide variety of hardware?
- Has a standard machine-interface been used?
- Is it possible to secure additional critical or essential functions?
- Have the systems to which data will be exchanged been specified?
- Has a generalized subsystem (interface) been specified for the interaction of data with other systems?
- Have standards (nomenclature, coding, structure, and so on) been used for the interaction of data?
- Have standards been used for the connection between hardware and infrastructure components?
- Maintainability influences the connectivity regarding the technical system architecture (see checklist for maintainability).

- How can users outside the native delivery environment access your applications and data?
- Does the system provide efficient application integration options to work with other back-end systems? Is there a description of integration architecture, including APIs, and where integration is tightly and loosely coupled?
- Does the system support industry standard data interchange standards, such as Polaris, EDI, and so on? Have you outlined data interchange standards supported and how data transformation occurs?
- What software design, development integration, and testing standards are used by the system?
- Have all the interfaces, including external ones, been identified and described?
- Are all the components interfaces defined?
- Does the integration strategy covers all the technology landscape including legacy platforms and existing applications, such as NSM, Device Management, Voucher Management, ALEPO, ERP, OIC, ODS, EDW, CWS, EAI, and so on?
- Is the architecture appropriately layered and can be realized through SOA?
- Does the system provide efficient application integration options to work with various systems; for instance, file systems, databases, applications, and so on?
- Does the integration architecture defined and describe an integration map?
- Are key capabilities like BPM, registry and repository, business rules identified and described?
- Does it leverage SOA principles and reference architecture?
- Does it support industry standard data interchange standards?
- Are e2e component interactions described?

Data domain

The following is the domain checklist:

- Does an organization-wide data model exist in which the system data are integrated with the company data?
- Is the logical data model specified?
- Do the data match the data model at the organizational level?
- Is the data model normalized?
- Is the data model parameterized?
- Is the data encrypted?

Infrastructure domain

The following is the domain checklist:

- For the benefit of the internal connectivity, have infrastructure components been used which are geared to infrastructure already in use?
- Is there a current infrastructure in use?

Robustness

The degree to which the information system proceeds as usual even after an interruption.

Business domain

The following is the domain checklist:

- Are the essential functions of the information system shielded in a separate subsystem?
- Are well-trained substitutes on stand-by within the production organization?
- Are well-trained substitutes on stand-by within the user organization?
- Have provisionsbeen made so that, in case of serious disturbances or disasters, the information services may continue as much as possible?
- Is a plan for disasters available?
- Is the user organization's level of dependency on the information system stated (critical, sensitive, non-sensitive)?
- Has the maximal tolerable time of breakdown been stated?
- Has it been determined what constitutes a disaster?
- Is a co-ordinator assigned in case a disaster occurs, and are the authorities and responsibilities determined for such situations?
- Have the emergency procedures and the alternative procedures for a possible transition period been described? (Amongst other aspects, attention needs to be paid to procedures handling unfinished transactions at the point of breakdown.)
- Does the plan for disasters include possible alternative hardware?
- Is, as part of the plan for disasters, a plan for an alternative location available?
- Have the organizational aspects been described, including the procedures for an alternative location?
- Has it been established which functionary is authorized to decide to make use of alternative computers?

- Has a similar production environment been reserved, for instance, in an alternative computer centre, including accompanying procedures for alternative use?
- Does the (external) executive organization responsible for the implementation of the alternative use have an up-to-date plan for alternative use?
- Is the plan for disasters known within the relevant organization departments? Will the plan for alternative use be tested periodically, but at least once a year?
- Will the findings of the test of the alternative computer use lead to amendments in the plan for alternative use?
- Will a test of the plan for alternative use take place after a major change in the system architecture?
- Have manual procedures been prepared in order to substitute (parts of) the automated information services?
- What level of reliability and accessibility is predicted for the system?
- How fault tolerant is the system and what are the fault handling strategies and procedures?
- Is the architecture well organized and have you provided a system overview, background information, constraints, and a clear organizational structure for all downstream designs?
- Have you identified approved performance targets, at a high level at least, with key stakeholders?
- Have you considered targets for both response time and throughput?
- Do your targets distinguish between observed performance (that is, synchronous tasks) and actual (that is, taking asynchronous activity into account)?
- Have you assessed your performance targets for reasonableness?
- Have you appropriately set expectations among your stakeholders of what is feasible in your architecture?
- Have you defined all performance targets within the context of a particular load on the system?
- Checklist for Architecture Definition
- Have you identified the major potential performance problems in your architecture?
- Have you performed enough testing and analysis to understand the likely performance characteristics of your system?
- Do you know what workload your system can process? Have you prioritized the different classes of work?
- Do you know how far your proposed architecture can be scaled without major changes?

- Have you identified the performance-related assumptions you have made (and validated them if needed)?
- Have you reviewed your architecture for common performance pitfalls?

Application domain

The following is the domain checklist:

- Are automatic alternative facilities built in?
- Have check processes (watchdogs) been applied?
- Will the data processing be done dually?
- Is the operator able to supply status information?
- Has the consistency of data been taken care of by use of checkpoint/restart utilities?
- Is the essential functionality stored in separate modules?
- Are the subsystems distributed?
- How is the technology designed to cater for current and future transaction loads?
- How does the system cater for user errors and mistakes?
- Are the component/module descriptions sufficiently described?
- Have the alternative designs been considered?
- Does the design put emphasis on reusable aspects?
- Are design decisions and assumptions documented explicitly and motivated?
- Does the design support proceeding to the next development step?
- Does the design emphasize simplicity?
- Does the design create reusable components where appropriate and emphasize reusability?
- Have known design risks been identified, analysed, and planned for or mitigated?
- Does the design emphasize the leveraging frameworks and libraries to facilitate maintainability and reuse?
- Does the design define and describe the class diagrams, sequence diagram and various modules in sufficient level of details?
- Are all the components interfaces defined and described?
- Is the entity model/domain model documented?
- Is a requirement traceability matrix included as part of the design document?
- Is error handling, logging and exception handling described?

- Are the NFR requirements addressed by the design document; for instance, security, availability, and scalability?
- Does it describe the tools and procedures for building, testing, and deploying the application/packages?
- Business continuity and recovery considerations
- System monitoring considerations
- Availability considerations

Data domain

The following is the domain checklist:

- Is the data storage distributed?
- What are the processes that standardize the management and use of the data?
- What business process supports the entry and validation of the data, and the use of the data?
- What business actions correspond to the creation and modification of the data?
- What business actions correspond to the deletion of the data; is it considered part of a business record?
- What are the data quality requirements required by the business user?
- What processes are in place to support data referential integrity and/or normalization?
- Has the database access been optimized?
- Are the tools or instrumentation that monitors the health and performance of the system considered?
- Are tools used for software, patches, bug fixes distribution considered?
- Is the instrumentation for application that allows for the health and performance monitoring described?
- Data Storage and Retention Considerations
- Quality Assurance Considerations

Infrastructure domain

The following is the domain checklist:

- Have hardware, network, PCs, system software, and DBMS been chosen which are geared to one another and to the applications?

- Is a dual set of hardware, and so on available for alternative use?
- Have you mapped all the system's functional elements to a type of hardware device? Have you mapped them to specific hardware devices if appropriate?
- Is the role of each hardware element in the system fully understood? Is the specified hardware suitable for the role?
- Have you established detailed specifications for the system's hardware devices? Do you know exactly how many of each device are required?
- Have you identified all required third-party software and documented all the dependencies between system elements and third-party software?
- Is the network topology required by the system understood and documented?
- Have you estimated and validated the required network capacity? Can the proposed network topology be built to support this capacity?
- Have network specialists validated that the required network can be built?
- Have you performed compatibility testing when evaluating your architectural options to ensure that the elements of the proposed deployment environment can be combined as desired?
- Have you used enough prototypes, benchmarks, and other practical tests when evaluating your architectural options to validate the critical aspects of the proposed deployment environment?
- Can you create a realistic test environment that is representative of the proposed deployment environment?
- Are you confident that the deployment environment will work as designed?
- Have you obtained external review to validate this opinion?
- Are the assessors satisfied that the deployment environment meets their requirements in terms of standards, risks, and costs?
- Have you checked that the physical constraints (such as floor space, power, cooling, and so on) implied by your required deployment environment can be met?

Auditability

The ease with which the correctness and completeness of the information (in the course of time) can be checked.

Business domain

The following is the domain checklist:

- Do programmed checks on the results of the data processing exist, such as control totals and square counts?
- Will transactions be numbered subsequently and is reference made to these transaction numbers in the mutation logs?
- Will report pages be numbered subsequently mentioning the total number of pages?
- Will historical data and mutation records be recorded and saved?
- Do retrieval functions with sufficient selection possibilities exist regarding the historical data?
- Do possibilities exist related to an audit trail?
- For the benefit of the audit trail, will mutations be recorded, who did it, and using which function?
- What are the data entity and attribute access rules, which protect the data from unintentional and unauthorized alterations, disclosure, and distribution?
- What are the data protection mechanisms to protect data from unauthorized external access?
- What are the data protection mechanisms to control access to data from external sources that temporarily have internal residence within the enterprise?
- Legal and Regulatory Considerations?
- Reporting and Management Information Considerations

Application domain

The following is the domain checklist:

- Do functions exist to check the correctness of the data?
- Do functions exist to check the completeness of the data?
- Will all transactions be registered, that is, logged?
- Have you described the system security architecture?
- How is the system protected? What are the physical, software, and human elements of this protection?
- What security products are used to protect the system?
- How is individual user system access controlled?
- How are individual users authenticated?

- How is system process authorisation implemented?
- How is individual user access control created and maintained?
- How is data protected?
- What security audit and control processes are in place?
- What security audit processes and procedures have been implemented?
- How do you monitor system security?
- What level of access granularity is provided?
- Does the security model support role-based authorisation?

Data domain

The following is the domain checklist:

Do possibilities exist for a (periodic) check of the data consistency?

Flexibility

The degree to which the user may introduce extensions or modifications to the information system without changing the software itself.

Business domain

The following is the domain checklist:

- Have you defined how flexibility requirements influenced the specified functionality and how it is distributed between the subsystems?
- Does the functional specification explicitly describe how future changes to the system should be implemented to preserve flexibility?
- Does the system use data coded for data entry, error handling, or information messages?
- How does the system personalise the user experience?
- Does the system provide any disability access support?
- How straightforward is customization and configuration?
- Is the architecture designed to accommodate future changes?

- Does the architecture avoid unnecessary redundancy? Have the following been considered as part of the approach?
    - Rationalization
    - Consolidations
- Is the architecture independent of the technology stack that will be used to implement it?
- Are architecture decisions and assumptions documented explicitly and motivated?
- Are there any missing or incomplete capabilities and/or components?
- Have known design risks been identified, analysed, and planned for or mitigated?
- Are components well-defined, including their functionality and their interfaces to other components?

Application domain

The following is the domain checklist:

- Have the programs been parameterized?
- Are logical values used instead of hard coded values?
- Has the data processing been separated from the data retrieval?
- Is it possible to modify (combinations of) input functions in order to change a way of work?
- Is it possible to modify (combinations of) control functions in order to change a way of work?
- Is it possible to modify (combinations of) processing functions in order to change a way of work?
- Is it possible to modify (combinations of) output functions in order to change a way of work?
- Is it possible to tune menu structures?
- Is it possible to change the contents of the input screens?
- Is it possible to change the layout of the input screens?
- Is it possible to create a selection of output data?
- Is it possible to change the layout of the output?
- Will code customisations hamper future software releases?
- Does the package allow different database and server technology options?

- Does the software support multi-company, multi-division, and multi-currency environments? Are there any restrictions to this type of environment?
- What data standards are used in the system design and operation?
- Can the system efficiently accommodate NU interface standards including look and feel, branding and corporate web site style?
- What is the strategy and architecture for expanding system capacity and how is this handled by the package? This should cover both application, database and infrastructure level scalability approaches, that is, scale up, distributed, scale out.
- Define the number of users the system can service and how different volumes are handled and managed. What are the maximum number of concurrent users, transaction through put, system load?

Data domain

The following is the domain checklist:

- Has the data model been parameterized?
- Has the data model been normalized?
- Has the normalized data model been implemented without changes?
- Do several search keys exist for each entity?
- Does a metadata model exist?
- Has a relational data structure been used?
- Is it possible to specify different search trails?

Infrastructure domain

The following is the domain checklist:

- Are 4GL facilities used?
- Can the user organization define reports easily?
- Have hardware, network, system software, programming environment, and DBMS been selected that are appropriate for the application concerned and that fit to the rest of the infrastructure?
- Have hardware, network, PCs, system software, and DBMS been chosen that are tuned to each other and to the applications?
- Has an objective definition been made for the quantity of processing capacity needed by the information system (centrally or decentrally) to match all functional and quality requirements?

Portability

The diversity of the hardware and software platforms on which the information system can run, and how easy it is to transfer the system from one environment to another.

Application domain

The following is the domain checklist:

- Have the programs been parameterized?
- Have applied national and international standards been used, e.g. for the exchange of data via networks (OSI, TCP/IP, XML), of applications in the IBM-environment (SAA), or of a standard programming language which can be compiled on a wide variety of hardware?
- Has a standard machine interface been used?
- Have possible machine dependencies been implemented in separate modules?
- Have the algorithms been optimized?
- Are the subsystems distributed?

Data domain

The following is the domain checklist:

- Has the approach of the database been optimized?
- Is the construction of the data programs (rules of integrity) independent of a specific DBMS (applied with client/server systems)?

Infrastructure domain

The following is the domain checklist:

- Have 4GL facilities been used?
- Have commonly used tools for development been used?
- Will a commonly used infrastructure be adopted?
- Has a standard programming language that can be compiled on a variety of machines been used?

- Has an infrastructure (hardware, network, and so on) been selected that is upwards compatible within a certain range?
- Has a commonly used infrastructure been adopted?

Reusability

The degree to which parts of the information system, or the design, can be reused for the development of different applications.

Business domain

The following is the domain checklist:

- Has a general reference model been used?
- Have the functions been modelled with a company business process model?
- The reusability is influenced considerably by the maintainability of (part of) the information system (see checklist for maintainability).

Application domain

The following is the domain checklist:

- Have applied national and international standards been used, for instance to exchange of data via networks (OSI, TCP/IP, XML), of applications in the IBM-environment (SAA), or of a standard programming language that can be compiled on a wide variety of hardware?
- Have the programs been parameterized?
- Has the data processing been split up into sub-transactions?
- Have the input, the processing and the output been implemented separately?
- Have possible machine dependencies been implemented in separate modules?
- Have I/O operations been arranged in individual modules in order to separate the retrieval of data from the processing of data?
- Has a standard machine interface been used?
- Have standard actions been built into the interface consistently?
- Have program modules been reused?
- Have the algorithms been optimized?

Data domain

- Does the data match the organization data model?
- Has the data model been parameterised?
- Has the approach of the database been optimized?

Infrastructure domain

The following is the domain checklist:

- Is a current infrastructure in use?

Testability

The ease with which the functionality and performance level of the system (after each modification) can be tested and how fast this can be done.

Business domain

The following is the domain checklist:

- Has the choice for subsystems been motivated?
- Is open, consistent, and up-to-date functional documentation available?
- Is the resulting testware completed and preserved for the benefit of future tests?
- Do tools for planning and defect management exist in support of the test process?
- Does a strong interaction or effect exist between the several functions?
- What system testing and implementation services are provided?
- What user testing environments are provided?

Application domain

The following is the domain checklist:

- Have standards for development been used (e.g. standard scheme techniques, standards for structured programming, standards for database approach, recognizable nomenclature, and standards for the use of user interfaces)?
- Have check processes (watchdogs) been applied?

- Is the operator able to supply status information?
- Is the data processing split up in sub-transactions?
- Have the input, the processing, and the output been implemented separately?
- Have possible machine dependencies been implemented in separate modules?
- Has the essential functionality been stored in separate modules?
- Have I/O operations been classified in individual modules in order to separate the retrieval of data from the processing of data?
- Are program modules reused?
- Have the programs been structured and are they easy to understand?
- Is open, consistent, and up-to-date technical documentation available?
- Are the subsystems distributed?
- Will the data processing be done dually?
- Have the programs been parameterized?
- Have the algorithms been optimized?
- Can test data be easily restored?

Data domain

The following is the domain checklist:

- Is the data encrypted?
- Has the data storage been distributed?
- Has the data model been parameterized?
- Has the approach of the database been optimized?

Infrastructure domain

The following is the domain checklist:

- Is an integrated test facility available?
- Will test tools be used, for instance for test execution or test planning and control?
- Is it possible to perform queries regarding the datasets?
- Does a separate test environment exist?

- Will an integrated functional development environment be used: Workbench (CASE-tool), word processor, and so on?
- Will an integrated technical development environment be used (modern development environment linked/integrated with a DMBS)?
- Will a code or system generator (ICASE) be used?

Accessibility

The ease with which end-users access the system.

Business domain

The following is the domain checklist:

- Does the UI design address compatibility with different web browsers including but not limited to Chrome, IE, and Firefox?
- Are the user volumes for various systems addressed by the architecture?
- Is there a strategy for expanding system capacity, and how is this handled by architecture?
- Are interface standards including look and feel, branding, and corporate web site style considered?
- Are the fault handling strategies and procedures described?
- Error handling, exception handling, logging, instrumentation
- Has the personalization aspect been defined and addressed by the architecture?
- Does the software support multi-company, multi-division, and multi-currency environments? Are there any restrictions to this type of environment?

Application domain

The following is the domain checklist:

- Are the error messages clear?
    - Yes
    - No (please indicate screen number and provide description)
- What is your opinion of the icons used (if relevant)?

- What is your opinion of the terminology on the screens?
- Did you notice screens in a negative manner?
  - No
  - Yes (please define what you did not like)
- Explanatory remarks: (also for the next questions)
- What is your general opinion regarding the screen layouts?
  - Unacceptable
  - Acceptable with adjustments
  - Acceptable
  - Does the system help you how to restore error situations and how to proceed?
- Are the help screens and help texts clear? What is your opinion on the use of them?
- What is your opinion about the use of the mouse?

- What is your opinion about the user documentation? In other words, to what extent does the user documentation really support working with the information system?

- What is your opinion about the start-up procedure?

- What is your opinion about the use of the function keys and buttons?

- Do you want more standardization for menu screens, function screens, function keys, buttons, and so on?

- What is your opinion about the menu structure? Do you want user menus?

- Are the function names clear to you?

- To what extent do the functions meet the way of working and the structure of the user organization?

- What is your general opinion about the layout of the reports?

  - Unacceptable
  - Acceptable, with adjustments
  - Acceptable

- Did you notice reports in a negative manner?
  - No
  - Yes (please define what you did not like)
- What is your opinion about the standards regarding the headers and footers of reports?
- What is your opinion about the print facilities?
- Do the reports contain the information wanted (are there too many or too few details)?

Closing thoughts

Software quality attributes are a critical factor in the longstanding success of any enterprise. Quality attributes increase organizational profitability, reduce maintenance cost, achieve loyalty, and customer fulfillment. Quality audits help ensure that the software achieves value and efficiency. However, it is crucial to perform software quality audits in a consistent and planned manner. These audits should be carried out throughout the SDLC, to verify and validate artifacts produced at the end of the various SDLC phases. Effective quality audits should not only focus on process conformance, but also incorporate software architecture, design, build, and testing to improve confidence in software quality.

Audit and accountability

Every stakeholder involved in an IT initiative must be held responsible for meeting the quality-attribute requirements. The process should be rolled-out, publishedm and understood by all the key stakeholders. Quality audits are not only held to find defects or nonconformance but also to promote the software-quality understanding within the engagement team. Before starting any quality checks, the approach, and the methodology should be communicated to top management, software architects, and software engineers so that everyone understands what the audit entails and how deficiencies will be detected and communicated. In addition to helping the audit process, this also provides stakeholders with an opportunity to think through ways of improving quality throughout the SDLC.

Architecture reviews and risks

Reviewing application architecture is a critical task in order to reduce the cost of errors and find architectural issues at an early stage. Architecture reviews are a proven, effective way of reducing costs and the probability engagement failure. Review architectures frequently: at major milestones of the engagement, and in response to significant architectural changes. Software architects should consider building the review questionnaire in cognizance, both to optimize the architecture and to reduce the time required for future reviews. The main goal of the architecture review is to determine the viability of the baseline and target architectures and to ensure that the architecture correctly establishes functional requirements and quality attributes for the target solution. Additionally, it helps to identify areas for improvement and recognize potential issues in the software architecture.

Scenario-based architecture evaluations is a powerful methodology for reviewing software architectures. In a scenario-based architecture evaluation, the focus is on the scenarios that are critical from a business standpoint, and which have the highest impact on the target architecture.

Leverage one of the following common review methodologies in tabular format:

Method	Description
Architecture Tradeoff Analysis Method (ATAM).	ATAM helps review architectural decisions with respect to the software quality attributes, and how well they satisfy the specific quality goals.
Active Design Review (ADR)	ADR is best suited for in-progress architectures. The main difference is that the review is more focused on a section of the architecture at a time, rather than a general overall assessment.
Active Reviews of Intermediate Designs (ARID)	ARID combines the ADR aspect of reviewing in-progress architecture with a focus on a set of issues and the ATAM approach of scenario-based reviews focused on quality attributes
Cost Benefit Analysis Method (CBAM)	The CBAM emphasizes analyzing costs, benefits, and schedule aspects of architectural decisions.

Audit and business objectives

The goal of **Quality Assurances (QA)** is to find defects as well as to validate that the software meets the business requirements, including software quality requirements, that is, NFRs. However, often, QA programs are actually aimed at functionality verifications and not quality attributes. This falls short of the real goals and objectives of an efficient QA program. The QA process that does not cover quality attributes is potentially incomplete.

NFR Quality Assurance	Application Performance Management / EMM
Combining software quality audits into testing programs provides an assurance of the software quality. All quality attributes specified in the technical specification should be tested. Only through such thorough testing can the stakeholders gain a level of confidence in the quality of the software.	APM is not end-user monitoring but part of the IT infrastructure and tools that are divided over many LOBs and stakeholders. These are different areas of the landscape that are monitored through a combination of different tools. The critical part is correlating the information from different sources within the application landscape and creating a single glass pane view for an enterprise which is also part of APM monitoring scope.
Testing Phases: Usability, internationalization, compliance, portability, recovery, reliability, maintainability, security, stress, volume, load, scalability, performance	Monitoring and Management: Real user monitoring, synthetic monitoring, application monitoring, business activity monitoring, database monitoring, mainframes, infrastructure servers monitoring, network, role-based dashboards

NFR measurement

Summary

Software quality is best achieved in the early stages of the SDLC when the cost to remediate is orders of magnitude less than it would be during operations or deployment phases. It is judicious to find and rectify defects as near to their point of origin as possible. Therefore, the quality audit should happen as early as possible in the software-development life cycle. Normally, a software-development life cycle is composed of many phases, starting from inception, requirement, architecture and design, development, testing, deployment, and operations. Exceptions and errors can occur at any point in the SDLC; and therefore, a rigorous quality audit program should be run in parallel with the engagement SDLC.

This final chapter of the book has provided summary and trends for the NFR domain. This also outlines architecture assessment and audit methodology.

Index

K

L

M

Printed in Great Britain
by Amazon